THE
NETHERLANDS

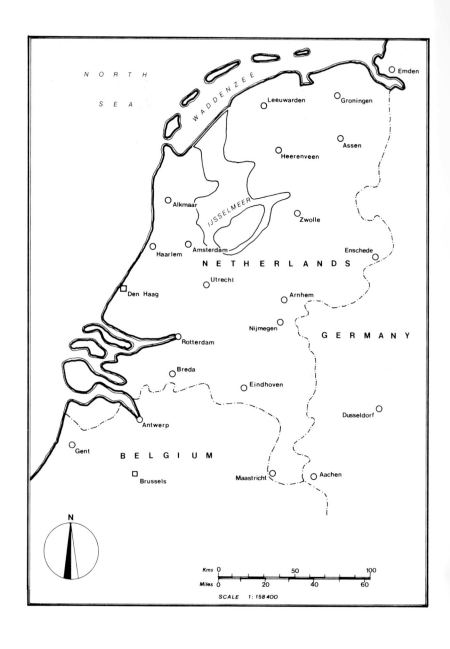

N O R T H

S E A

W A D D E N Z E E

Emden

Leeuwarden

Groningen

Assen

Heerenveen

Alkmaar

IJSSELMEER

Zwolle

Haarlem

Amsterdam

Enschede

N E T H E R L A N D S

Den Haag

Utrecht

Arnhem

Nijmegen

G E R M A N Y

Rotterdam

Breda

Eindhoven

Dusseldorf

Antwerp

Gent

B E L G I U M

Brussels

Maastricht

Aachen

N

Kms 0   50   100
Miles 0   20   40   60

SCALE   1 : 158 400

THE
NETHERLANDS

NINA NELSON

B. T. BATSFORD LTD · LONDON

To Peggy and Oliver

© Nina Nelson 1987
First published 1987

ISBN 0 7134 5170X

Typeset by Servis Filmsetting Ltd, Manchester

Printed in Great Britain by
The Bath Press
Bath, Somerset
for the publishers B.T. Batsford Ltd
4 Fitzhardinge Street, London WIH OAH

Contents

Acknowledgements

The Netherlands, although a small country, is so rich historically and there is so much to do and see that, even with all the help that I was given, it is unlikely that I have covered all the ground without omissions.

I have been fortunate in being assisted by many knowledgeable people. Giedie Bierens, Director of the Netherlands National Tourist Office in London, and Marcel Baltus had the answers to my questions. Augusta van Berckel of the Netherlands Board of Tourism in Leidschendam pointed me in all the right directions and made further contacts easy and fruitful. Els Wamsteeker of the Amsterdam VVV found accommodation at the height of the tourist season and ensured that I saw everything in her city. Throughout my travels I had only to follow the signs to the VVV in each place and tell them what I was doing; immediately all the information was made available and I am most grateful to them.

I am indebted to various associates. Among them Dick Back in Nijmegen; Pim Lening in Rotterdam; Jan Kappenburg and Jitti Jaarsma of Groningen VVV; Paul Borchert at Schiphol; John de Canha in Amsterdam and James Holloway, a fellow travel writer who knows Holland well.

One of the things which made my task so much easier is that everybody seems to speak English. It is a great comfort to be able to pick up the phone and get help from the operator in your own language!

Grateful thanks go to the following for permission to reproduce photographs: Herbert Felton: 25; Foto-Reclame: 14, 17; A. F. Kersting: 4, 7; Lichtbeelden Instituut: 15, 20; NBT: 1, 18, 19, 22, 23, 24, 26, 30, 31, 34, and colour 1–4, 6; Rijksbureau voor de Monumentzenzorg: 21; Vroomdelingenverkeer: 36, 37; VVV: 3, 5, 6, 9, 10, 11, 12, 13, 16, 32, 33, 35, and colour 5; A. D. Nelson: 2, 8, 27, 28, 29.

I

HOLLAND YESTERDAY AND TODAY

Countries do not usually have two names but the Netherlands, meaning low lands, are also called Holland, literally the hollow or marshy land. The inhabitants are called Dutch, a corruption of the German Deutsch, perhaps implying that many Hollanders and Germans come from low lands. It is only seven times larger than Prince Edward Island in Canada or little more than one-and-a-half times the size of Wales. Yet during its Golden Age in the seventeenth century it became one of the great world powers. When it broke out from beneath the Spanish yoke a period of exploration and commerce ensued, and the Dutch East India Company was formed. Dutch merchantmen sailed the world. The Netherlands had territories in the East Indies and smaller holdings in South America – Dutch Guiana and Curacao – and their ships brought back silks and spices from those places to Europe. It was not only to the Far East and Africa that they went but also to North America, where New Amsterdam (New York) was founded. Prosperity brought more leisure and, in its wake, cultural pursuits.

Wedged between Belgium, Germany and the North Sea the Netherlands comprises 11 provinces and measures only 210 miles (336 km) from north-east to south-west and 30 miles (48 km) east to west at its narrowest part. But although it is so small a country, it boasts many unusual features. The rivers, confined between man-made earth banks, sometimes flow several feet above the surrounding countryside. One-fifth of the land lies below sea level and the threat of floods and gales means constant vigilance. More than half the population lives on land which could easily be flooded at high tide if there were no dykes to prevent this.

There is a saying that 'The Lord made heaven and earth but the Dutch made Holland.' Certainly they take their unrelenting struggle with the ocean as a matter of course. The Zuyder Zee is no more. By throwing up a 20-mile (32-km) dam to cut off the North Sea, engineers have turned it into a freshwater lake. In turn this lake has been pumped dry section by section creating fertile land and villages called *polders*. Buildings rest on piles driven into the mud. This method has been used since it was discovered long ago that certain hardwoods will not rot if they remain submerged.

Such stupendous undertakings have left an indelible mark on the Dutch character. They are a practical, efficient, but cautious people. One of their maxims, 'Don't go on the ice after one night's frost', typifies their caution. Yet they can also be daring and welcome anything new. Although great individualists, as a nation they have a common determination to quell and wrest a living from the sea. They enjoy life at a leisurely pace and prefer to entertain at home rather than in restaurants. Education is of the highest level, family life closely knit, the housewife economical. They are very hospitable and languages come easily to them – most speak two or three. You can drive anywhere and the police usually understand what you ask them in English and direct you on your way.

From William of Orange to Queen Beatrix

In Renaissance times the Netherlands comprised a few duchies, cities and countries loosely knit under the crown of Spain. When King Philip II would not condone the spread of Calvinism, introduced sterner tax measures and overrode local laws, the outraged nobility rallied behind William of Orange and voiced their grievances. Philip, never renowned for his diplomacy, ignored them and the situation worsened. In Spain the Inquisition was in full spate and the Spanish decided that heresy must also be quelled in the Netherlands. Rebellion broke out in Holland.

William the Silent, son of the Count of Nassau, was born at Dillenburg in Nassau and succeeded in 1544 to the small principality of Orange near Avignon in southern France. He is one of the most outstanding figures in Dutch history, and, although referred to as the father of the Netherlands, he is more often known as William the Silent, which is perhaps another way of saying 'diplomatic'. He was prudent, well educated, far above the average in intelligence and, unlike most of the wealthy young princes of his day, industrious. He moved from his ancestral estates in Germany to oversee other estates his father had gained in the Netherlands and championed the rebellion against King Philip. He was considered a Dutchman because of his holdings in the Netherlands and, owing to his obvious ability, the Dutch nobles were quite prepared to let him act for them. An excellent conversationalist, he had the enviable gift of making everyone feel at ease.

The wealthy merchants were uncertain where they should put their money. They had flourished under Spain but, when the Duke of Alba imposed a fresh 10 per cent sales tax, they volunteered their backing to the House of Orange. Fighting continued for the next ten years. William sold his gold and jewels while his brother, John of Nassau, pledged his estates. Sometimes the Dutch won; at other times the Spanish. The Dutch gained a victory at Heiligerlee in Friesland, but were then defeated

at Jemmingen and so the triumphs went to and fro. In 1567 William went
to Nassau to plan ahead and bide his time. He wrote to his brother 'With
God's help I am determined to go on'.

In September 1568 William crossed the Meuse with 18,000 infantry
and 7000 cavalry, but the Spanish refused to be drawn into open warfare
and William, through lack of money, had to disband his forces. It was a

1 *To many young tourists this is essentially the Netherlands — the combination of
windmills and bicycles*

miserable time for the Prince. He went from place to place in fear of assassination and creditors. His wife, Anne of Saxony, left him.

Religious tyranny was anathema to William, but to identify himself with the struggle to remove the Spanish yoke he made a public profession of his Calvinist faith. He stipulated three conditions to put affairs back to normal in the Netherlands.

1 Freedom of worship and liberty to preach the gospel according to the word of God.

2 The restoration and maintenance of all the ancient charters and privileges and liberties of the land.

3 The withdrawal of all Spaniards and other foreigners from all posts and employments civil and military.

William's private life was scarcely less dramatic than his public one. His second wife, Charlotte of Bourbon, was recovering from the birth of a baby when William was shot at by a half-witted clerk employed by a Spanish merchant. The bullet went through his right ear and out by the left side of his jaw. Medical science at the time could not successfully treat such a wound. His doctors could only advise pressing a lint pad to the hole to staunch the flow of blood. For several weeks Charlotte insisted on doing this herself without rest and, just when the Prince began to recover, she died of exhaustion.

Once again William was left with children and no wife. His next choice was wise. He married Louise de Coligny, daughter of a Huguenot French Admiral, and moved to Delft where a large monastery was converted for him. It was from Delft that he directed the relief of Leiden after that little town had suffered many months of siege from a Spanish force.

For some days in July a stranger was observed outside the Prince's home. When questioned he said he was a Frenchman, Balthazar Gerard, only surviving son of a family which had been massacred for being Calvinists. This untrue story had been thought up by a priest who had convinced the Frenchman that it would be a virtuous act to assassinate the Prince and had absolved him in advance of the sin he was about to commit. Nobody disbelieved Gerard and he was even allowed to visit William in his bedroom so that he might tell the tale of the Prince's good friend, the Duke of Anjou, who had died of tuberculosis.

Gerard was seen on 8 July in one of the hallways, but again had a good answer. He was on his way to church where the Prince was to attend a service that morning. As the church was across the canal in front of the Prince's residence, the explanation was accepted. Someone did point out that it was strange that the Frenchman had used the back door, but Gerard replied that his clothes were so old that he was ashamed to show himself at the front entrance. On being told this the Prince generously sent him some money to buy clothes before returning to France.

The money was used instead to buy two pistols. A further request was sent to the Prince to write a letter of safe conduct so that Gerard would be allowed to return to France without interference from Dutch officials. He was told he would receive the pass on the afternoon of the next day, 9 July. On that afternoon he duly presented himself at the monastery. Princess Louise saw him and, startled by his expression, rushed to her husband and said that she did not trust Gerard. William reassured her with the words 'Merely a poor devil of a French refugee. An honest Calvinist and one who has suffered much for his faith.'

The burgomaster of Leeuwarden in Friesland had lunch with William that day. His name was van Uylenborch and he was the future father-in-law of Rembrandt. As the Prince was leading his guest from the dining room along a corridor, he paused at the bottom of a staircase. Gerard leapt out from a hiding place and fired both his pistols directly at the Prince. One of the bullets went through a lung and the other into his stomach. He fell dying on the steps. His Master of Horse rushed to his aid and held him in his arms. The Prince whispered 'Oh Lord have pity on my soul and upon these poor people.'

William's son, Maurice of Nassau, was to bring his father's dream of liberating the Netherlands to fruition. He was a natural soldier and leader, and the independence of the Republic was finally agreed at the treaty of Munster in 1648.

William II, Prince of Orange, was born at The Hague in 1626 and married Mary, Princess Royal of England, in the Royal Chapel in Whitehall. He was nearly 15, his bride five years younger. He had ambitious plans to reinstate his brother-in-law Charles II on the throne of England. Unfortunately he died of smallpox before he was 25 years old.

At the Congress of Vienna in 1815 Holland and Belgium became a united kingdom under William V's son, who took the title of William I of the new kingdom – which can make Dutch history rather complicated!

William I restored the House of Orange. His son became William II, and William III was the father of Wilhelmina, born in 1880. Queen Wilhelmina's reign is the longest in Dutch history. As she succeeded her father when she was only ten her mother, Queen Emma, served as Regent until her eighteenth birthday. After a reign of 50 years, Queen Wilhelmina abdicated in favour of her daughter Juliana in 1948.

You will often see an orange streamer attached to the Dutch flag (which has three horizontal stripes, red, white and blue); it expresses loyalty to the House of Orange.

Queen Juliana spent some years during the Second World War in Canada with her daughters, and Princess Margriet was born in Ottawa. As a memento of her sojourn, the Queen sends tulip bulbs to the

Canadian capital each spring. The flower beds surrounding the Government buildings in Ottawa are gay with tulips at this time, a charming reminder of the Queen's stay.

In 1980 Queen Juliana, like her mother before her, abdicated in favour of her eldest daughter, the present Queen Beatrix. The latter lives with her husband and three sons in a wooded area on the outskirts of The Hague in a palace, the Huis ten Bosch. Before her marriage the Queen spent four years at Leiden University. Annually, as Queen Juliana used to do, she opens Parliament on the third Tuesday in September at the thirteenth-century Knight's Hall in The Hague, arriving in a golden coach drawn by eight horses. It is a pageant which both local people and visitors love to watch.

Hofjes

The Calvinistic spirit has much to do with the Golden Age of the seventeenth century. In Pieter de Hooch's house interiors one can glimpse growing signs of wealth in the elaborate furniture and tooled leather walls. It was a time of tolerance and prosperity. Descartes went to Holland to escape interference, and rather bitterly announced that the people of Amsterdam were so busy making money that they left him alone. He was not so scathing about the artists and sat for Franz Hals. Of Vermeer he said that his scenes of Delft showed not only the light of Holland, but also 'the natural light of the mind'.

A lasting and remarkable benefit of the seventeenth century is the *hofje*. As is well known, Dutch families are particularly devoted and the problems of the elderly members were solved by building *hofjes* in every town. It is a misnomer to call them alms houses because they are not strictly for elderly poor people. Wealthy families clubbed together to make these charming places which consist of small houses surrounding a square with gardens. Sometimes a building will accommodate several people, sometimes one or two. Occasionally there are two-roomed flats. The gardens are well kept, nurses and doctors are available and the elderly live in dignity, paying rent according to their means. Religious organizations and family trusts sustain many of them, and coats of arms decorate the entrances.

No stigma is attached to spinsters, widows or other aged folk who enjoy these quiet retreats, and visiting relatives have no guilt complexes about the charming living conditions. The houses are usually single-storey, thus saving stair-climbing, for in Holland staircases are notoriously steep. A few *hofjes* are arranged for married couples. Those who cannot manage to run their own quarters are looked after, but most manage with a little help. *Hofjes* function throughout the country, and

2 Hofjes

whether they are in a picturesque seventeenth-century square or an ultra-modern district, the way of life seems to suit everybody.

St Nicholas

During the seventeenth century Dutch ships trading along the Mediterranean coasts brought the St Nicholas story back from Spain to Holland and from there the Dutch settlers took it to America. In the United States Sinter Klaas eventually became Santa Claus and his feast day changed from 5 December to Christmas Eve, probably due to the Reformation, which emphasized religious celebrations at Christmas time. However, the feast day has never changed in Holland and the giving of gifts to children is still observed on the night of 5 December, and 6 December is a holiday.

St Nicholas was a dearly-loved bishop whose generosity to children was well known, and word of this spread to many countries. On his feast day he traditionally visits children and brings presents. In return children write poems for him and leave them in their empty clogs beside the sitting room fire place. The Saint is accompanied by Spanish blackamoor servants in medieval costumes. They are called Black Peters and carry bundles of switches for beating naughty children. St Nicholas is pictured as a white bearded old gentleman in bishop's red robes and gold mitre, carrying a shepherd's staff.

In Amsterdam, St Nicholas' Church is named not only after the traditional protector of children but also because St Nicholas is the patron saint of sailors. Each December a parade, led by a St Nicholas with his entourage of Black Peters, marches to the Royal Palace. There is then a discussion with the Mayor about the children's behaviour during the preceding year. The Saint assures him that they have been well behaved, wishes the onlookers a happy Christmas and tells the children that he will visit their houses later that night to deliver presents. Bags of sweets and gifts are duly posted through front doors and hallways and, after the parcels are opened, the family sit down to a table covered with Christmas fare: chocolate and pastry letters filled with almond paste, cakes and various kinds of sweetmeats.

The Dutch are great sticklers for the correct food at appropriate times. In their armed forces *Rijstaffel* is a favourite meal on feast days and there is a tradition in the Navy that it is served for lunch twice a week, on Mondays and Thursdays. It is an Indonesian meal, not unlike an Indian curry with rice, forming the basis for a variety of spicy dishes.

When the Dutch sailed to the East Indies they brought back not only spices and silks, but many intriguing oriental customs and designs in jewellery and wearing apparel. Rich merchants copied the Persian habit of draping tables with silken shawls and rugs, and today many restaurants still cover their tables in the same way.

Traditional costumes

There are several places where people still wear colourful costumes; towns such as Volendam, Marken and Scheveningen and also isolated villages on the islands of Zeeland, Hindelopen – once a flourishing seaport in Friesland – and Staphorst in the eastern part of the country. These traditional costumes differ from village to village – even the clogs do – and in Marken, particularly, there is an oriental flavour. The cottons and chintzes used on the exotic dresses have Indian designs.

Staphorst
At Staphorst the women wear silver helmets from which dangle golden spirals like plastic curls. Their bodices have large collars decorated with painted flowers and the skirts are blue and black striped with strange

3   *Traditional costumes as worn by girls in Marken*

padded hips. On Sundays wooden clogs are replaced with black leather shoes with enormous silver buckles.

The men look dull in comparison in black jackets and trousers, although the former are brightened up with double rows of silver buttons and large silver watches hanging from silver chains. Their heads are covered by flat tam-shaped caps. Small boys wear skirts until they are three years old and little girls have their hair brushed up over their caps.

If you are fascinated by these colourful trappings you must not take photographs in Staphorst. Visitors are not welcome and certainly not photographers. Tourists have had their cameras knocked out of their hands. Other Dutch villages welcome strangers and are only too pleased to pose for amateur photographers, but Staphorsters are isolationist to a degree. They resent outsiders, Dutch or foreign, and only marry amongst themselves.

These people have a saying 'No farmer can buy a cow until he is sure of the calf' and their courting procedure bears this out. It is rather like the Welsh 'bundling'. Bedroom windows are not difficult to reach and a suitor can climb up a courting ladder to his intended's room, but on the first occasion he must leave one leg dangling over the sill for all to see! If the girl's parents approve of the match, they will allow the young man to climb in. Otherwise he is pulled out by the legs.

Staphorst is a close religious community (all illnesses are viewed as being the will of God and must be tolerated as such) and the people are staunch Calvinists. On Sundays, they file into church with hands clasped and eyes turned to the ground, carrying the family bibles fitted with shining brass edgings in their right hands. Those in mourning wear blue. After the service they remain indoors and prefer not to venture out except on foot. If you do feel tempted to visit this beautiful village, with its stunning display of ancient costume and architecture, it is best to avoid a Sunday.

Religion

The Dutch Constitution guarantees complete religious freedom and equality of rights regardless of creed. Yet Protestant and Catholic are still sharply divided and there is an old Dutch saying that when you have one Dutchman you have a theologian, two Dutchmen a sect and three a schism. Although these days there is great tolerance, each side tends to stick to its own faction. The only indication to the visitor is that Protestants wear wedding rings on the third finger of the right hand. This can lead to confusion as a plain ring often doubles as an engagement ring, which Protestants wear on the left hand and Catholics on the right.

Weather

The Netherlands has a maritime climate with cool summers and mild winters. Here is a table showing the average temperature and hours of sunshine a month.

14.2

	Av. temp °C	°F	Av. hrs of sun	Rainfall in mm
January	1.9	35	51	64
February	2.3	36	71	48
March	4.9	41	128	49
April	8.4	47	157	48
May	12.4	54	214	52
June	15.2	59	218	62
July	17.2	63	210	81
August	16.7	62	205	83
September	14.2	58	148	68
October	9.8	50	102	68
November	5.5	42	51	77
December	2.4	36	42	74

Communications

As canals are always associated with Holland and as there are over 3000 miles (5000 km) of navigable waterways, one is inclined to forget that there are also excellent roads, all well signposted. The motorist will find that even the so-called secondary roads have good surfaces and, in the north of the country, the motorways are delightfully free of traffic. It takes only about six hours of easy driving to get from the north to the south of the country and less than four hours from the Hook of Holland to the German frontier. The bicycle is still the Dutchman's favourite means of transport.

Since the landscape is generally flat with only an occasional hill, then if you too are a keen cyclist, Holland is for you. Bicycles are the main means of transport and it is said that 14 million people own about 11 million bicycles. Whether this is an exaggeration or not, the first thing the visitor is conscious of when driving a car in traffic is innumerable cyclists.

If you favour this form of transport, bring your bicycle across the Channel with you. Cycling maps are available from most VVV offices and give you routes and picturesque tracks where cars are prohibited. It is as well to remember that the prevailing wind comes from the south and south-west, so it is easiest to cycle with the wind rather than into it. For instance, the coastal route from the Hook of Holland to Den Helder is quicker and easier if you start from the former.

The legendary figure of the Flying Dutchman has become a reality in a sense, for the creation of KLM (Royal Dutch Airlines) was the remarkable work of a pilot, Albert Plesman, who was born in The Hague in 1889. During the Second World War the Dutch Far Eastern offices operated independently and KLM planes, left in Britain when the Germans overran Holland, linked Bristol and Lisbon. Plesman himself ran a flying school in Holland and kept air personnel up to date, but he was later interned by the Germans. Within months of the end of the war Plesman had KLM flying again. He managed to persuade President Truman to make over 18 C54 Skymasters to Holland. He became president of the International Air Transport Association in 1948 and remained as head of KLM until his death in 1953. KLM's main office in The Hague has as its address 1 Plesmanweg and it was he who coined the phrase 'the air ocean unites all people'.

Land reclamation

Land reclamation is a subject that every Dutchman enjoys discussing. In what other country is there a Ministry of Water? Their great concern is keeping the sea at bay. Almost 20 per cent of the land surface of the

Netherlands has been reclaimed, and there are some fascinating examples. An outstanding one is Schiphol Airport on the outskirts of Amsterdam. Even though ultra-modern today, it celebrated its sixty-fifth birthday on 17 May 1985, for the first plane arrived there in 1920 from Croydon. Fifteen feet (4.5 m) below sea level, Schiphol lies on the bottom of what was once Haarlem lake, a place renowned during the Eighty Years' War (1568 – 1648) for a naval engagement between the Spaniards and the Dutch. Surely it must be the only airport ever built on the site of a sea battle.

Early in their history the Dutch acquired skill in making canals and building dykes. To begin with, coarse grass was grown to bind sand hills together and, when the water overflowed, they were strengthened and raised. Later willow bundles were plaited about stakes and joined together to make mattresses which were weighted with rocks and sunk into position. This technique has never been bettered and is still used to bolster dykes. Once a ring embankment has been made the water is pumped out, which is where the windmill took over in the old days. As the sails turned they moved a large scoop which gathered up the water and spilt it into canals. Thus were created the famous *polders*.

Nowadays miracles are wrought with concrete piles, pier cradles, sluice gates, computers and hydraulic engineering. Dutch expertise has spread to other countries and, besides endless work in Holland, there are large exports of bridges, jetties, water moving equipment and ships. Although land reclamation goes along at a terrific pace, so does the population growth. Holland is one of the most densely populated countries in the world and its people have the longest life expectancy, averaging 71.4 years for men and 74.8 for women. Statistics show that Holland has proportionally more young people than any other country in Western Europe. About 38 per cent of the total population is under 20 years of age.

Government

Although Amsterdam is the capital of the Netherlands, The Hague, the third largest city, is the diplomatic centre, the seat of government and, once again, the Royal Residence. The powers of the sovereign are limited by the constitution. Executive power is in the hands of the cabinet but requires the support of a parliamentary majority. The cabinet cannot govern if parliament is opposed to it.

The legislature, the *Staten General*, has two houses. The lower house, or second chamber, has 150 members, elected by popular vote using a system of proportional representation. The upper house, or first chamber, comprises 75 members elected by the *Provinciale Staten*

(Provincial Representative Councils). The first chamber votes on bills passed by the second chamber. The *Provinciale Staten* are elected in the same way as the second chamber. The municipalities, which have a large degree of financial and administrative autonomy, are governed by municipal councils elected by direct popular vote. The mayor or burgomaster, who is chairman of the municipal council, is appointed by the Queen upon the recommendation of the government. The Queen signs bills passed by parliament. Each governmental act requires the joint consent of both the Queen and that member of the cabinet whose department is concerned with the act; the signatures of both will appear on the relevant royal decree.

The International Court of Justice occupies the most important building in The Hague. It is a city of broad avenues, stately palaces and gabled mansions. The old part of the town is charming with its thirteenth-century Binnenhof, the former castle of the Dukes of Holland, and the Royal Art Gallery, the Mauritshuis, with its paintings by Rubens and Rembrandt. Between The Hague and Scheveningen there is the miniature town of Madurodam.

Various towns and districts

The nearby seaside resort of Scheveningen has been completely redeveloped and is now the prime bathing resort of the North Sea coast. Particularly interesting are the Gevers Deynootplein (a square in Scheveningen) with the Kurhaus, Circustheatre and the Boulevard. The northern part of the latter with its terraces and shops is called the Promenade and is only accessible to pedestrians.

Amsterdam is unique, consisting of 90 islands joined together by some 550 bridges. The buildings rest on the tops of thousands of piles driven into the sea bed so that in effect it sits on a giant forest. A series of concentric canals, dug more than 300 years ago, encircle the centre of the city.

Amsterdam, with its neo-baroque buildings and churches, is never more lovely than when seen from one of the glass-topped boats which pass silently along the waterways. Of the many words used to describe it, Erasmus phrased it very aptly by saying he 'knew a city in which people lived like crows in the tops of trees'.

The Dutch are proud of their heritage of great paintings by such masters as Rembrandt, Rubens, Hals, Van Gogh and Vermeer and nowhere can these be seen to better advantage than in Amsterdam's Rijksmuseum. Probably no other artist in history has won such a wide and enduring popularity as Rembrandt. During the 1630s, when his reputation grew and orders for portraits were numerous, he still found time to paint subjects of his own choosing and to experiment with the best methods of reproducing rich fabrics, various textures and the interplay of light and shade. The Rijksmuseum has his most famous painting, *Night Watch,* a large canvas with life-size figures of merchant soldiers, which he completed in 1642.

For those who are serious museum addicts the Museum Ticket is an economical buy. It gives entry to some 16 museums in Amsterdam and dozens more around the country. The tickets are issued at VVV offices and save not only money but time. An added benefit for those under 25 is that they pay only half price.

To the north of Amsterdam and the west of Ijsselmeer are the flower-growing districts. During the third week of February each year you can see the largest and most beautiful bulb show in Europe. The love story of the Dutchman for the tulip is a romantic one. It is said that the tulip was imported from Turkey during the sixteenth century and the richness of its colour and graceful form started a mania for the flower. New varieties were carefully bred which were so expensive that not only money but houses, horses and coaches, antiques and other items were bartered in exchange for an exotic tulip. The flower soon had a Stock Exchange value. After 1636 the Dutchman and his tulip settled down to a more mundane existence; but, despite the other lovely flowers grown by him, he has remained faithful to his first love.

Each town has its own speciality. Haarlem, the capital of North Holland, is the centre of the bulb district. It also has one of the finest squares in the country, the Grote Markt. Delft has an annual antique dealers fair and the famous china is made there. Limburg offers caves and grottoes; Friesland has farms and lakes galore, and Eindhoven, home of the giant Philips Company, boasts a mighty mushroom. It is a concrete dome 252 ft (77 m) in diameter, rising 98 ft (30 m) into the air, and was built in 1966. Alkmaar has an open-air cheese market which is held every Friday morning from May to October. Cheese porters wearing the traditional white costume of their guild weigh thousands of cheeses on huge scales.

Gouda is the rival to Alkmaar with its cheese market. Here market day is on Thursdays and bargaining goes on in front of gaily-painted farm wagons laden with orange-coloured cheeses. It is sometimes claimed that William Shakespeare was buried in Gouda. To add force to this statement it is pointed out that he was a Roman Catholic and he could have fled to Holland during the Church reform in England and, taking another name, lived in Gouda. It is also said that when he was dying in 1617 his Dutch friend William Cool offered him a place in his family tomb in St John's church. In the meantime, people continue to visit the tomb in Westminster Abbey.

4 *The Town Hall at Gouda*

St John's church has been likened to Chartres and has magnificent stained-glass windows, one of which was given by William the Silent. Next to the church, in the municipal museum, there is an exquisite gold chalice presented to the Society of Archers by Countess Jacqueline of Bavaria in 1465, which is said to be the finest in the world. Gouda's elongated clay pipes are renowned and at one time the making of these was a flourishing trade. In wintertime, a feat attempted down through the years is to skate from a town about 12 miles (19 km) away, like Rotterdam, to Gouda, buy a pipe and return all the way with it clenched in one's mouth without breaking it.

The canals and lakes do not always freeze over in the winter. However, when they do, there are ice skating races whose origins stretch back hundreds of years. Whole villages turn out to watch and cheer the skaters on as they skim along the canals and afterwards there is feasting and drinking to celebrate. The most famous race is run through eleven towns and is called the Eleven Town Race (Elf Steden Tocht). Starting at 7 a.m. it ends after dark, for the course covers over 100 miles (160 km). The participants stop at various hostelries for food and drink to help them on their way.

Exchange

Visitors often wonder why in Holland the guilder is written as Fl, the abbreviation for florin. It stems from the seventeenth century when the florin replaced the guilder by order of Emperor Charles V of Hapsburg. Officially the monetary system was still based on the guilder, which was eventually reinstated, but the sign Fl has remained its symbol. The guilder is divided into 20 stuivers (5 cent coins) or 10 dubbeltjes (10 cent coins) or 4 kwartjes (25 cent coins). Two and a half guilders make one rijksdaalder, the slightly larger 2.50 coin. Paper money comes in the following values: 5 green, 10 blue, 25 red, 50 yellow, 100 brown and 1000 dark green.

A small commission is charged for cashing travellers cheques but you will get a better rate than for bank notes. However, commission can vary considerably, especially in Amsterdam, and so you would be well advised to 'shop around'. For uniform Eurocheques there is no charge. Credit card holders can obtain cash advances. There is a large network of *bureau de change* offices, and many of them have extended opening hours. In some coastal resorts you can change money at the VVV offices.

Tips for travellers

When booking in at a hotel you are not usually asked to leave your passport as in some other countries, but you merely show it so that the number can be entered on your booking form. Room prices normally include breakfast and, in Holland, this is quite a meal.

Many of the large hotels in Amsterdam are in the city centre and visitors often do not realize that about 20 minutes by car or public transport would bring them to the outskirts, where, to the south and west there are garden suburbs. Here you will see many fine buildings, high blocks of flats, modern houses, wide streets, tree-lined avenues, shopping centres, canals and parkland. Tunnels and flyovers facilitate commuter traffic at rush hours.

Most taxis are ordered by telephone even at hotels. If you try to wave one down when shopping or sightseeing it usually sails past, probably *en route* to someone who has ordered it. It is possible to hire one at a taxi rank. They have a small sign on the roof. There is an extensive network of public transport in Amsterdam. Fares are cheap and you can buy day tickets for use on the whole system.

Whatever else your suitcase contains be sure to pack walking shoes useful for sightseeing and essential for the cobbled streets. A light raincoat is a must as you can expect the occasional shower at the least. Men are expected to wear jackets in the better restaurants, though not always a tie. Suits for men and cocktail dresses for women are required for formal occasions, but on the whole clothes are informal. In summer, something warm for the shoulders is useful for the ladies. Bathing suits are normal, unless you prefer one of the naturist beaches along the North Sea coast, and of course there are topless places. With warm outfits for winter and light clothes for summer you cannot go wrong, but spring and autumn can be capricious so have a light coat or wrap of some kind.

English newspapers and magazines are available countrywide, as are books. There are radio and television programmes in English and of course you can get the English radio services.

Electric current is 220 volt 50 cycle AC. Plugs are of the Continental type, different from both US and UK. If you do not have your own adaptor you may be able to borrow one from the hotel desk.

The Netherlands Board of Tourism

The Dutch Tourist Offices are scattered throughout the country and could not be more helpful. Their official name is difficult to pronounce – Verenigin Voor Vroomdelingenverkeer – so they are known universally as the VVV (pronounced Vay Vay Vay). When driving through the country you will notice as you enter each town, among the travel signs, an inverted pale blue triangle with the letters VVV and an arrow. Follow these signs and they will lead you to the local office, often situated near the railway station. The staff always seem to speak English and will help you with leaflets, maps, and suggest places to stay. The Head Office is at 5 Rokin in Amsterdam and there are three information centres in Amsterdam: one at 10 Stationsplein opposite the Central Station (open from 9 a.m. to 11 p.m. in summer), another at Leidsestraat near the Leidseplein, and a third on Rijksweg A2 near the entrance to the city. They provide an accommodation-finding service for a small charge for those who arrive without reservations.

Car hire

Self-drive cars are relatively inexpensive. *Right* is a word to remember when driving, for three reasons: you drive on the right; vehicles coming from the right have right of way and, if turning left at a junction where there is an island or police pedestal, leave it to your right. The wearing of seat belts in the front seats of cars is obligatory, and there is a general speed limit in built-up areas of 30 mph (50 kmh).

Many of the streets in Amsterdam are very narrow because a canal often runs down the centre. In addition cars are parked facing the canals

5 *Car parking in Amsterdam. Only a thin, metal rail is there to prevent cars from plunging into the canal – is it any surprise that so many cars have to be rescued from canals!*

on either side. Add to this the inevitable bicycle and you have a traffic problem second to none. It is not uncommon for cars to end up in the canals, but fortunately most are not very deep and guard-rails line many of them. There is a rescue organization called the Amsterdam Voluntary Rescue Brigade with over 3000 members. These gentlemen will willingly instruct you about what to do if your car plunges into the water. The main point to remember is that if you cannot save yourself, go into the canal boldly! The car may then land upright and have more chance of floating. Some other points are: do not panic; do not try to open the car door immediately; let water seep in even if it means opening the window slightly. When the pressure has equalized internally and externally you can open the door and swim out. It is more than likely that a member of the Brigade will have been alerted by this time. The Fire Department has a special crane for lifting vehicles out of canals. There is a small fine if you indulge in these aquatic activities.

Entertainment

The high standard of Dutch opera and theatre is internationally acclaimed. Amsterdam's Concertgebouw is world-famous. Who has not heard of Holland's most gifted conductor, Bernard Haitink, sometimes called Britain's favourite Dutchman? He is musical director designate of London's Royal Opera and for many years has been chief conductor at Glyndebourne. Tickets for the Concertgebouw are difficult to obtain and, despite the fact that people are seated actually on stage to left and right of the orchestra, it is a favourite place for international artistes to perform.

The Stadaschouwburg in Leidseplein is Amsterdam's Covent Garden. Ballet and plays as well as opera are performed here. Its atmosphere extends out over the pavement with overhead arches and a large chandelier. The ballet is known not only for its classic presentations but for its *avant garde* approach.

The Hague has its own philharmonic orchestra which gives concerts in the Congress Centre containing three theatres and a concert hall. In June there is a festival with international ballet, opera and plays.

Entertainment can be found in all the main cities. Night clubs are numerous and daring. Striptease shows take place in cabarets and intimate bars. The drug scene seems almost tolerated and gay clubs are easy to find. As many change their locations frequently and the police keep an eye on things, they are difficult to name. The well-known places are usually acceptable to most visitors, but it is advisable to avoid the less salubrious areas. The VVV are helpful but, if you want something more daring, your hotel porter or taxi driver may prove more helpful.

2

Amsterdam

Schiphol

Schiphol is one of the most up-to-date airports in Europe, handling millions of passengers annually, many of them inter-changing between airlines for further travel. Should you arrive for a visit to the country in late spring or summer, when emerging from customs and awaiting a taxi, do not be surprised if you catch the scent of flowers on a breezy day. Although delightful it is not an illusion. Rose bushes flourish along the banks of shallow canals near the airport buildings and car parks. Nearby is the striking aluminium dome of the national aviation museum. Here, if you have time to spare and are interested in aviation, you can trace the history of flight from the Wright brothers' exploits to the present day. Just a two minute shuttle bus ride will take you from the terminal to the Schiphol Hilton where you will again detect the scent of roses, for the grounds surrounding it are laid out with flower beds.

Flowers have always been associated with Holland and cover more ground than grass. Great quantities are carried for other nations to enjoy. British Caledonian alone has a million pound contract to transport them daily to New York. They are cut and packed in dry ice each morning, flown from Schiphol to London Gatwick, and transferred to the transatlantic flight arriving, thanks to the time difference, in New York that same afternoon.

Most of the main Dutch towns are within easy reach of Schiphol. It is 25 miles (40 km) from The Hague (45 minutes by coach), 39 miles (62 km) from Rotterdam, 24 miles (38 km) from Utrecht and 63 miles (100 km) from Arnhem. You can reach the centre of Amsterdam in under 30 minutes and Amsterdam Central Station is now connected by a rail link to the airport.

A line of tax free shops stretches the width of the airport so you are bound to pass through at least one. They are reputed to have the lowest prices of any continental airport as well as being the largest tax free centre in Europe. Amongst the many things on offer beside the inevitable liquor, tobacco and perfume, are cameras, binoculars, typewriters, tape recorders, lighters, leather goods, transistor radios, pewter, golf balls,

6 *The port of Amsterdam is not yet the largest in the world – that is the port of Rotterdam – but it is the most modern in the field of container transport*

television sets, tulip bulbs, cheese and, most astonishingly, motor cars. This last provision is aimed primarily at the North American tourist and most of the cars are left-hand drive. The organization will arrange to ship your car home at the end of your continental tour if you hand it back to them at the airport. The showroom has a choice of models, and, within half an hour, you can drive away from the airport in your new vehicle complete with documents and licence plates.

Schiphol is probably the first *polder* (land won from the sea) visitors step on in Holland. The word *schiphol* means ship hole or haven and it is the clue you have that this ultra-modern airport is built on reclaimed land below sea level. It is not unusual for passengers to be astonished when they see the sails of boats on nearby canals above their own level.

Amsterdam is compact, beautiful and welcoming. It is easy to find your way round after a day or so, and English is spoken everywhere. Early Dutch settlers who canalized and lived along the Amstel river built a huge dam whose site is now the heart of the city called Dam Square. A network of canals and streets encircles it. The Royal Palace edges one side. It was formerly the Town Hall built by Jacob van Campen in 1648. To the right of it is the New Church and to the left the Bijenkort (Beehive), Amsterdam's most famous shop. This large department store has entrances from both the Dam Square and the main shopping street, Kalverstraat. Its many floors are choc-a-bloc with everything from leather goods and furniture to cosmetics and food. There is a special service counter which will arrange overseas delivery for anything you may care to buy, and a very good restaurant which gives an excellent view over the Royal Palace and the Dam Square. There is also access from the Damrak, a wide thoroughfare which leads to the Central Station past the Produce Exchange and the Bourse. Opposite the Royal Palace on the other side of the square is the famous Krasnapolsky Hotel.

Krasnapolsky Hotel

The Grand Hotel Krasnapolsky is rightly described as having a romantic past and an exciting present. Its name is associated with Amsterdam in

7 *The Royal Palace and the Dam*

the same way as Shepheard's Hotel was with Cairo. Its foundations are on the spot where a dyke once held back the river. Early in the seventeenth century a road was built on this dyke which is still called the Warmoestraat. It owes its name to the market gardens which originally lay at the foot of the dyke. This road gradually developed into one of the most fashionable in Amsterdam. Distinguished merchants built their mansions and spacious shops along it, and behind these dwellings ran the Damrak, the mouth of the river Amstel, from which Amsterdam (Amstel Dam) takes its name. It was the city's principal harbour before it was filled in and made into the broad street it is now. It is difficult to realize today that at one time you could stroll along its length and see ocean-going vessels returning from long and dangerous voyages to the East Indies or the Levant. Here they moored and unloaded their costly merchandise into cellars or had them hauled up into the lofts of the merchants' houses on the hoisting beams. It was in this street that the Netherlands' Shakespeare, Joost van den Vondel, lived, at number 111. A small statue marks the spot.

By the next century the wealthy merchants built more mansions overlooking the city's canals – Prinsengracht, Keizergracht and Heerengracht – and on the scene appeared a Polish tailor named Krasnapolsky. He was a genial, far-sighted young man and did so well in his trade that he was able to buy a little café in the Warmoestraat. It stood on the site which is now occupied by the hotel which still bears his name.

Krasnapolsky was a born hotelier. Handsome, well dressed and determined to please his customers, his café soon became renowned as the meeting place of merchant captains, naval officers and stock dealers. Beer and coffee were the only beverages served, but during the second half of the nineteenth century it became the fashion to sip a glass of wine now and again. Krasnapolsky began to import wine which he bottled himself and, to build up his stocks, he rented cellars under the city pawn shop. These vaults were ideal and had once belonged to the fourteenth-century Magdalene Convent not far from the present Town Hall.

Wine drinking was heady and to offset its effect Krasnapolsky thought of a novel idea – to serve pancakes made by his sister-in-law, Mathilde. To this day pancakes in the Grand Hotel are baked '*à la* Mathilde' and they became a Dutch speciality, not only in the hotel – where it is thought that over two million had been served before the last war – but all over Holland.

Krasnapolsky's business flourished and he extended his café into a restaurant by buying adjacent houses. Another of his dreams was soon realized. He decided to build a glass hall, decorated with flowering plants and trees where, however inclement the weather, his clients could enjoy the illusion of sitting out in the sun to enjoy their meals. His Winter

Garden was unusual at that time and not only were his regular customers delighted but he began to build up an international reputation.

To make himself independent of local flower growers he bought a nursery north of the city and grew his own palms, ferns and flowers. He added hotel rooms to his restaurant in 1880 and so the Grand Hotel Krasnapolsky was born. As long ago as 1883 his rooms were centrally-heated, electrically lit and had parquet floors, the first of their kind in Holland. In the *Mirror of the Sea* Joseph Conrad describes the Winter Garden thus:

> A gorgeous café in the centre of the town. It is an immense place, lofty and gilded, upholstered in red plush, full of electric lights and so thoroughly warmed that even the marble tables felt tepid to the touch. The waiter who brought me my cup of coffee, by comparison with my utter isolation, had the dear aspect of an intimate friend.

Krasnapolsky had earned enough money by then to take over the first Amsterdam Electricity Company, which enabled him not only to fit his hotel with ultra-modern lighting but also to help with the festivities at the fortieth anniversary of King William III's accession to the throne. The citizens of Amsterdam gasped with pride when he provided the Dam Square with a fairy-like illumination of no fewer than 500 bulbs, an unheard of way to celebrate at that time. He died at the age of 78 in 1912 and, although his only son died some years before he did, his lovely Winter Garden is still enjoyed by guests and his name lives on in one of the most pleasant squares in Europe.

Some years ago the then manager, Mr de Boer, told me many amusing stories about the hotel. One of his nicest concerned two Mexicans who booked into the hotel on a bitterly cold winter's day. They had not been to Europe during the winter before and, as they had no overcoats, were delighted to be shown into their centrally-heated bedroom. When the question of going out of doors again arose, one of them had a brilliant idea. He decided that, as the rooms were so warm, there was no need for the rose-coloured blankets on the beds. He suggested to his companion that they would make excellent ponchos and, with a pair of nail scissors, cut a hole in the centre of each blanket. And so two warmly-clad Mexicans went out shopping. 'Of course,' ended Mr de Boer, 'we don't usually encourage guests to behave like this or we would soon have no furnishings left!'

Dam Square

From the front windows of the hotel the sculptured pediment of the Royal Palace across the Dam Square can be seen to its best advantage. The scene depicted in this triangular space, just below the open belfry, shows sea creatures cavorting around King Neptune. Built as the Town Hall in 1795 – one great chamber was known as the largest room in Europe at the time – it was turned into a palace for Napolean's brother, Louis, who lived there for 18 years. He furnished it in Empire style and several magnificent pieces still remain. It was often referred to as the eighth wonder of the world because its foundations were made by driving 13,659 wooden piles through yielding mud into firm clay.

The War Memorial to the valour of the Dutch people during the Second World War stands in the centre of the Dam and consists of a simple plinth flanked by statues and 12 urns. Each one contains soil from different places, one from Indonesia and others from the 11 provinces of the Netherlands.

Amsterdam in the fourteenth century consisted of the Dam with its large square and rows of buildings contained within a crescent-shaped canal. Just beyond the canal, at the head of the old harbour, was the Weeping Tower where sailors' wives waved farewell to their men. It is now inland, but one wonders if anyone waved goodbye to Henry Hudson or what they thought when he sailed past the Weeping Tower. This Englishman made voyages to discover the North-East and North-West Passages, first for the Muscovy Company and then for the Dutch East India Company. When he sailed past it in 1609 it was to explore the river in the New World which was named after him. On his last voyage he discovered Hudson Bay, but then his crew mutinied and set him adrift in a small boat. He vanished and was never seen again.

As Amsterdam grew, a web of canals spread out from the Dam Square. The city's numerous picturesque waterways are crossed by more than 500 bridges, many of them such as the Blue Bridge, with supports shaped like the prow of a ship.

The Begijnhof

Leading off the Dam Square along the Kalverstraat – Calves' Street, for it used to be the cattle market – with its enticing shops, you will pass an outstanding Renaissance gate which was once the entrance to a monastery; it is number 92. Carry on down the Kalverstraat and between numbers 130 and 132 there is a very narrow side street called the Beynensteeg. Walk down its length to a gate at the end. Go through this and you will be back in the Middle Ages in an old square. Silent houses and gardens surround it. Trees bend over wrought iron railings and in the centre there is a small church with a slender steeple. You are only some 60 ft (18 m) away from the bustling Kalverstraat, yet it is so quiet you might be in the countryside. You are in one of the quaintest squares in Amsterdam, the Begijnhof.

8 *The Dam*

This was originally founded by the Sisters of St Begga – a saint who died in AD 690 – who came from a village near Amsterdam in 1346 and formed a community called the Convent of the Beguines, or the Sisters of the Blessed Sacrament. They built their convent in the city to be near the Miracle of Amsterdam, the story of which has an unpleasant beginning.

A man lay dying in a house situated close to the land where the Sisters had set up their community. As he approached death he was given Holy Communion, but he was unable to swallow the bread and regurgitated it into a bowl which one of the sisters held for him; she then threw the contents into the fire place. The next day when she rekindled the fire she saw the consecrated bread, white and untouched, rising above the flames. She placed it on a clean cloth, laid it in a chest and rushed out to announce the news. The bread was taken to St Nicholas's Church but the following morning it was not there; it had reappeared in the chest. This happened several times, the story spread and many priests became worried. It was eventually taken as a sign by the clergy that God wished to be honoured more openly. The holy bread was returned to the church in the midst of a procession.

The miracle attracted much attention and the story was eventually written down and authenticated by the seals of the Bailiff of Amsterdam and the City Council. The Bishop of Utrecht went into the case thoroughly and gave permission for it to be made public. Special prayers of thanks were said. The house where the miracle had occurred was turned into a chapel called the Nieuwe Zijds, or Holy Site, but it suffered many vicissitudes. In 1578 it was confiscated by the city authorities and in 1908, in spite of protests from Roman Catholics and Protestants, it was demolished.

From that time the chapel of the Beguines became the Holy Site. A silent procession takes place each year on the anniversary of the miracle and is attended by many Roman Catholics.

The Begijnhof was a most unorthodox convent. The Sisters did not live together in one large building, but each by herself in a tiny house. These long lines of houses still form most of the square today. The Sisters met together only at their church and the rest of their time was devoted to good works and charity. Their life was strict and, although they lived alone, there were rules about buying a house or having a new one built. They did not take solemn vows and could retain and do what they wished with their personal belongings, but they were excommunicated if they broke any of the rules. No pets could be kept in the square, men were forbidden in their houses at night, nor could they themselves be away from them at night. Every evening both gates leading to the court were locked and this custom persists today.

After the Reformation the Beguines' chapel was confiscated and given to the Protestants, though they were allowed to remain in their houses. They were forbidden to attend Mass, but met secretly in a different house each day in case of discovery. After a time one of the empty houses was turned into a secret chapel. However, the desire for a real church remained and a compromise was worked out by their parish priest, the Reverend van der Mye, in 1655. He asked the City Council if he could buy two adjoining empty houses to transform into a chapel if he did not alter the outside appearance. Permission was given and a new secret church was added to the many that existed in Amsterdam at that time.

The church you see today was designed by a well-known architect called Vingbooms. The removal of the house ceilings long ago had left two galleries which are still supported by Tuscan columns. The nut-wood pulpit is carved with scenes showing the sermon on the Mount and the Transformation of Christ. Behind the altar there is a painting of the Miracle of Amsterdam and, to one side, a painting of a procession celebrating the Miracle. Above the altar is a crown presented by a most distinguished pilgrim, Maximilian, Archduke of Austria. During the last restoration of this little church stained-glass windows were designed by Gisele van der Gracht, giving what is thought to be a likeness of the original house.

When visitors come to the Begijnhof they often repeat a sentence which has been said many times before – 'Wouldn't this make a wonderful film set?' The square is not large yet it is surrounded by 164 houses. To one side of the centre stands the English Reformed Church like a Noah's Ark, with an apron of green lawn which was used in the old days for bleaching linen in the sun. The minute houses are mostly seventeenth- and eighteenth-century but, surprisingly, a few have fifteenth-century interiors. Their gables differ and this is emphasized by their proximity to each other. There are 'neck', 'clock' and 'step' gables. As house numbering is fairly recent there are gable-stone pictures to distinguish one from the other. These are mostly biblical scenes and are charming. As the houses are now numbered, it is easy to find the most interesting ones: 19 shows the Holy Family fleeing to Egypt; 23 has St John writing his gospel; 24 is of St Ursula, a favourite saint of the Beguines, and 27 has the Virgin Mary holding the Christ child.

You can visit the oldest house in Amsterdam at number 34. It is an enchanting tiny wooden dwelling some 500 years old. As the second floor is built out on consoles, the top of the house appears to jut forward and this adds to its attractiveness. The interior has pure Gothic lines and when it was being restored a painting was uncovered on a wooden partition which adds to the magic – it shows the Virgin Mary with a unicorn!

Next door number 35 has been made into the twentieth-century Orientation Centre for Foreigners. The interior of this little house was repaired in 1959 and the ground floor is fitted with counters where you can ask for information and buy books and postcards.

The English Church in this quiet enclosure has had an amazing history. It belonged to, and was used by, the Beguines for about 150 years and suffered greatly in the Amsterdam fires of 1421 and 1452. Each time it was rebuilt and enlarged. It is at least consistent that the church taken from the Beguines to prevent them saying Mass should have become a refuge for Puritan clergy driven from their livings in England for refusing to adhere to the Beguines' beliefs!

The first English minister was the Reverend John Paget from Cheshire. A document in the Consistory Room reads:

Anno 1607

In the year of our Lord and Saviour 1607 and on the fourthe daye of the moneth of February, after the new stile, about 4 of the clock in the afternoone, was the Church in the round Baguinhoff opened in the presence of Mijnheer De Schout (Sherriff) and D. (Domine) Petrus Plancius Minister of the Dutch Church att Amsterdam and att that present was the pulpitt brought in and set up for the use of the English Church att Amsterdam, publiquely erected by the consent of the honourable the Senate of the forenamed city: which their love and bountye towards us of the English nation the Lord repay unto them a thousand folde in this life and in the life to come with eternal happiness. Amen. The 5 of February following being the Lord's day betwixt 9 and 10 of the clock in the forenoone after prayer and thanksgiving to God for his mercy in this work begun, did Mr John Pagett (who was called to be pastor of this English Church) preach the first sermon in the aforesaid church and his text was psalm 51:10. Create in me a cleane heart O God.

John Paget had been installed by the chaplain of the British troops at Utrecht in the presence of members of the Dutch government. Some 68 British religious refugees and merchants became members of the congregation, but this increased so much that the church had to be enlarged yet again and the consistory and deacon's chambers were added.

Cornelia Arena, a devout Beguine, was grief stricken when one of her relatives adopted the new form of religion. Cornelia begged that when she died she should not be buried in an ordinary grave, but in the gutter by the north wall of the church so that the rain from the roof would always fall on her resting place as a sign of her sorrow. When she died, however, she was buried within the church, but the sexton found the grave open shortly afterwards and the coffin on its side. As with the Miracle of Amsterdam this phenomenon happened again and again until Cornelia's wish was granted. Yet her bones did not rest in peace for very long for the church was rebuilt once more in 1727 and her remains had to be buried closer to the garden. A stone marks the place and every year the youngest nun in the Beguine order lays a handful of sand and flowers on the spot.

The English Reformed Church, with its simple tower surmounted by a wooden steeple, has a spacious interior with a buttressed nave and wooden vaulting. Four flags give an inkling of its history. One represents the Scottish Mackay Regiment (which served in Holland from 1572 to 1582) and the others are the Union Jack, the flag of the House of Orange, and the Stars and Stripes. The latter was presented by the

Pilgrim Fathers from the port of Delftshaven who had taken refuge in Holland in 1608 and left for America in 1620.

The seventeenth-century pulpit has been decorated with four panels carved by Edema van der Tuuk to celebrate the accession of Queen Wilhelmina. The front panel is of an angel blessing the Dutch coat of arms and on either side of the church is portrayed as benefactress and teacher. The brass lectern was presented to the church by King William II of England and his wife Queen Mary when the King paid a visit to Amsterdam. The emblem is that of a lion and a lion's paw and the monogram is inscribed 'W.M.R.R. anno 1689'.

A few Sisters of the Beguine order lived out their lives there, but most are now occupied by self-supporting spinsters who form part of the parish presided over by the Dean of Amsterdam.

If you leave the Begijnhof by the same route chosen to enter it (that is along the narrow Beguinensteeg) you will pass two places where you can relax. The first is a minute restaurant called, appropriately, The Little Nun (Het Begijnje). It has leaded glass windows through which you can glimpse flickering candles, for even lunch is served by candlelight in this intimate place. Next to it, but less glamourous, is De Pilsener Club which, as its name suggests, is a public bar.

The Begijnensteeg leads back into the Kalverstraat which has some of the best shops in Amsterdam. Two of the well-known chain stores in Holland are called by their initials, V & D (Vroom & Dreesman) and C & A, named after two brothers, Clement and August Brenninkmeijer. C & A shops are such a part of British life that it is somewhat surprising to learn that this is an entirely Dutch enterprise.

Diamonds

Amsterdam shops are packed with luxury goods, and window shopping is a pleasant pastime for the Dutch are artists when it comes to such displays. Many shops are noted for distinctive china and glass, antiques, silver and gold ware and jewellery. Whenever one thinks of jewellery in Holland one's thoughts turn to diamonds, especially in Amsterdam. Surely its most fascinating industry must be diamond cutting and polishing and tourists seldom leave the city without visiting one of the well-known factories or exhibitions where the work is carried out.

Diamonds were discovered for the first time in India and stories of their scintillating beauty soon penetrated the far reaches of both East and West. From its discovery to being worn as adornment, the diamond's path is long but full of excitement. The mining of these precious gems is unusual in that they are always found as single crystals not attached to any matrix. Each diamond has a cleavage plane parallel to the octahedral faces, and this is used as a guide by the cutters to split off thin fragments in a definite direction. Due to its hardness the stone can be ground and polished only with its own powder. It is weighed in carats. The word 'carat' comes from the Greek word *Keration,* the fruit of the carob tree, of which 24 are supposed to equal 1 oz (28 g). Today a carat is taken as the equivalent of 200 milligrams.

The Dutch have been cutting and polishing diamonds since the late 1500s. It has become a traditional art and has always been concentrated in Amsterdam. Probably the most famous firm is Asscher's, whose main building is near the Amstel river. The business has belonged to the same family since about 1850 and the firm's Golden Visitors' Book has been signed by distinguished personalities from all over the globe. Among the signatures of Kings and Queens are those of Queen Elizabeth and the Duke of Edinburgh.

Asscher's have handled many internationally-famous diamonds, the largest one being the Cullinan which was named after the chairman of the Transvaal Diamond Mining Company. It was discovered in the early weeks of 1905. Its length was over 4 in (10 cm), it weighed 21 oz (600 g) – no less than $3024\frac{3}{4}$ carats – and it was sold for $150,000 to the South African Government who presented it to King Edward VII. The two Asscher brothers had a private audience with the King on 15 September 1907, and the cleaving and polishing of the great stone was discussed. The following year the Cullinan came to Amsterdam where police kept guard over the Asscher factory during the next few months while the stone was examined and plans discussed for its cutting. Joseph Asscher was to have the last word on this. After minute investigation he finally made up his mind where the cleavage was to be made. Everything depended upon the skill and judgement of the master cleaver. The result would be either the most fabulous gems or shattered remains. The suspense mounted as Joseph Asscher raised his arm and brought it down with a swift blow. The Cullinan split perfectly into two parts. No one said anything for a few breathless seconds. Then there was loud cheering and everyone had a stiff drink of *genever* (gin).

After careful manipulation the Cullinan yielded a magnificent collection. Cullinan I, pear-shaped and weighing $516\frac{1}{2}$ carats, was added to the British crown. Cullinan II, a four-cornered gem of $309\frac{3}{16}$ carats was placed in the Royal sceptre. The remaining diamonds were, of course, smaller but all sparkled with a strong blue-white fire, full of life. These magnificent diamonds can be seen and admired by visitors to the Tower of London.

Some time after the cleaving of the Cullinan Joseph Asscher was asked to speak about diamonds on an official occasion. He said:

The predilection for adornment which has animated all nations throughout the history of the world will only disappear with humanity itself. Who does not wish to wear a modest brilliant? Who does not wish to add a second to the first? When one is acquainted with the difficulties of cutting the stones, when one has learned to appreciate designing and the art of mounting: in a word, one's eye follows the long road from the depth of the mine to the jeweller's shop. It may safely be stated that wealth which consists of diamonds is beyond possibility of decline.

And it cannot be said that this wealth is unproductive for does it not bring, every day and unfailingly, dividends of joy, of happiness and of beauty?

Diamond cutting and polishing is fascinating to watch, especially when the work is explained step by step as it is in the various Amsterdam exhibitions. At the Asscher factory a colour film of the process is shown as well. First of all flaws must be eradicated before a rough diamond is cut. This is done by cleaving or sawing which takes ten hours or more for a small stone. Sawing is done by thin bronze discs coated with diamond dust. The pieces are then rounded by rubbing together, after which they are faceted.

Asscher's offer interesting advice about the care of diamonds. Only a diamond can scratch another diamond. The best way of avoiding this is by keeping jewels in separate protective containers such as chamois leather pouches. Settings should be examined from time to time for looseness, but never prodded. To prevent microscopic internal flaws from becoming enlarged, exposure to severe or prolonged cold or heat must be avoided. They can accumulate a harmless, but dimming, film from natural skin oils and dust, particularly when set in rings. A recommended cleaning method for modern jewels is as follows: place it in a solution of hot household detergent which can even be brought to the boil for ten minutes. Rinse in running hot water for several minutes and then dip in spirit or eau de cologne and rinse again. Then allow to dry in an absorbent material, such as a paper handkerchief. After a brisk brushing with a soft brush the diamond will shine like new. Antique jewellery, however, should not be treated in this manner and periodic cleaning is best left to your jeweller.

Tourist attractions

It seems incongruous, after looking at exquisite diamonds, within five minutes to be gazing at a merrily playing barrel organ, yet this can be done even in Amsterdam's smartest shopping quarter. These barrel organs have evolved from the early Hurdy Gurdy into quite sophisticated machines of considerable size mounted on a motor-driven cart. They

9 *Amsterdam, the town sung about by numerous artists, is full of music originating from the many beautifully carved barrelorgans*

are rented out and are big business for both owners and operators. Why this nineteenth-century craze has survived almost exclusively in Holland is not clear. They are largely extinct elsewhere in Europe and seem an anachronism in modern busy streets. They rival the teenagers' radios with the newest pop and delight the older folk with such standards as the Blue Danube and are much photographed.

Possibly part of the magic is because the instruments are kept in tune. The cherubs, puppets, bell ringers and other fantastic figures adorning them are always freshly painted and gleam gaudily in carnival fashion. Whatever the reason, the copper cups jingle with money as the organ grinders proffer them to clients. If their smiles are anything to go by they make a good living.

Also near the Dam do not be surprised to see girls wearing Scottish tam o'shanters and tartan kilts, waiting to cross the traffic-filled

10 *Amsterdam, seen from the building of the Netherlands Bank, is unsurpassed. Here it is easy to see the combination of the old with the new*

roundabout. The usual kilt pins have been replaced by miniature swords, decorated with the British Caledonian lion. These girls belong to the airline, whose main Dutch office, nearby in Rokin, is in one of Amsterdam's preserved historic buildings. Until recently a cat statue surveyed the scene from a pinnacle on the roof, seemingly symbolic of the airline's lion logo. Sadly, it had to be removed recently when it became insecure.

The Central Station is a great landmark – about ten minutes walk from the Dam along the Damrak – and was designed by the same architect as planned the Rijksmuseum. It is a remarkable building when you realize that its foundations consist of three artificial islands and 9000 piles, and it is used by 900 trains a day.

Not far from the station you can see the 223 ft (68 m) wooden tower of the Old Church, which was consecrated in 1306. It contains three beautiful stained-glass windows of biblical scenes by Pieter Aertsen and one showing the arms of the burgomasters of Amsterdam.

The city's coat of arms consists of a red shield with a black column containing three white St Andrew crosses, topped by an Emperor's crown. The latter was conferred by Maximilian of Austria in 1489 in gratitude for the city's support of the Burgundy-Austria dukes when they laid siege to Rotterdam and Woerden. The right to carry the crown ensured that Amsterdam was recognized everywhere as being under the protection of the Emperor. A replica of the crown adorns the 280 ft (85 m) tower of the Westerkerke, designed in 1638 by Jacob van Campen. The St Andrew crosses forming the letter X are the same shape as that on which the martyr, St Andrew, died. The two lions were added during the sixteenth century while the motto beneath was added on 29 March 1947, when Queen Wilhelmina granted the right to incorporate the words meaning Heroic, Resolute and Charitable. These acknowledge the heroism of Amsterdam during the German occupation from 1940 to 1945. Nowadays the crosses are often referred to as three kisses from Amsterdam.

Amsterdam is a magnet for drug addicts because of somewhat relaxed police control. It is perhaps wise to steer clear of certain sections at night. Mugging is not unknown and strip bars and clubs are on the make. Close by the Old Church is the red light (*rosse buurt*) district where sex shows and shops abound. The law forbids soliciting and girls may be seen sitting in windows seemingly uninterested in the passers-by who peer in at them. Part of this quarter can be seen from the tourist boats.

For newcomers to Amsterdam the best way of getting to know it is undoubtedly to tour the city in one of the glass-topped boats which glide quietly along the canals, round small quays and under low arches and bridges. They start from various places including Rokin near Spui. From these boats you can see the hoisting hooks projecting from top storeys in the old houses far better than when strolling along the streets. You might think that they are a meaningless relic of history, but they still have an everyday use. Dutch furniture, however beautiful, has always been heavy and cumbersome to lift. Even today such things as pianos, beds and dining room tables would never pass through the narrow seventeenth-century doors and windows and there is no question of carrying things up the unusually steep staircases.

You can receive the impression when looking up that whole rows of houses lean forward as if to admire their reflections in the canals in narcissistic contemplation. They are built this way so that when furniture and merchandise are hauled up to the lofts they will not scrape the walls.

You may still see what look like car rear-view mirrors on the walls of some houses. They enable the occupants to see who is at the front door

11 *A glass-topped tourist boat in Amsterdam*

without using the stairs. As many houses have been converted into flats, a glance in the mirror will often decide who the caller is likely to want. Again to avoid the stairs a basket can be lowered to a tradesman to transact business. The mirrors are not as popular as they used to be as they are ruination to late night doorstep romance!

At 26 Kloveniersburgwal is the narrowest house in Amsterdam which seems to be all staircase inside and is called The House of Mr Tripp's Coachman. Mr Tripp was a wealthy seventeenth-century merchant whose coachman once said in admiration of his master's house 'I'd be happy if I had a house as wide as Mr Tripp's front door'. Mr Tripp took him literally and built him the house you see today.

The housing shortage is acute in Holland particularly in Amsterdam. Many people live on houseboats moored in the canals and the number is supposed to be controlled at 1000, but there are at least 2000 – one of which is a home for stray cats! As you pass the latter you will see several

12 *A gabled house in Amsterdam*

well fed cats sitting on deck watching you or strolling about. One wonders who pays the food bill.

Each bridge you pass beneath is different and, if you take a candlelight evening tour, each is ringed with golden lights. One has iron barred windows set in the brick piers and served as a jail years ago. The Heerengracht canal is lined with elaborate seventeenth-century mansions, for here merchants strove to outdo one another with differently designed gables. The façades have carved plaques denoting the owners for whom they were built at a time when house numbers were not used. Along other canals you will see warehouses and smaller dwellings. As always in Holland flower pots and boxes abound, and there is even a floating flower market. The canal tours take about an hour, and at night, when the trip is more expensive, you are served with cheese and wine *en route*.

If you would like to explore the canals in an unusual way you can do so by hiring either a two or four seater pedalo. They are easily controlled and have awnings to keep off rain or sun. They can be hired from various moorings and you can enjoy a leisurely pedal along the canals for an hour or so.

One of the prettiest bridges in Amsterdam is near the Waterlooplein; it crosses the Amstel. Known as the Skinny Bridge it is very narrow and more than 200 years old. Its double drawbridge is still raised by hand. Waterlooplein, a square since 1880, was once part of a canal, long since filled in. It has always been a great tourist attraction because of its flea market. Both local and foreign buyers enjoyed shopping and bargaining there, but it has been temporarily moved to the Valkenburgstraat because of the building of the new Town Hall and Opera House. It will be moved back to the Waterlooplein when construction is complete.

Nearby is the Portuguese Synagogue, one of the largest in the world and said to be a copy of the temple of Solomon. In the early 1600s Portuguese Jews sought refuge in Holland during the Inquisition. The Dutch have always been noted for their religious tolerance and also gave shelter to the Pilgrim Fathers and the French Huguenots. The synagogue has not altered much since the seventeenth century and services are still conducted by candlelight. The philosopher Spinoza worshipped there. To the right of the synagogue stands an impressive statue of a dock worker by Mari Andriessen, a recent work marking the occasion in 1941, during the German occupation, when many brave Dutchmen stopped work in protest against the persecution of the Jews by the Nazis.

The Anne Frank House

The hiding place in the house at 263 Prinsengracht, where Anne Frank and her family lived, is a poignant reminder of those days of persecution and is now a museum. From the outside the house looks like hundreds of other homes belonging to merchants of modest means. Elongated high-ceilinged rooms, one on top of the other, are joined by a steep staircase. It is not until a bookcase is swung out from a landing to reveal the hiding place and you step through that the horror of those days asserts itself.

Otto Frank was a banker in Germany but left in 1933 when Hitler issued one anti-Jew law after another. Like so many men before him he sought refuge in Holland, and started a gelatine business in Amsterdam. Later he joined Peter van Daan, a specialist in the preparation of spices, as a partner in a spice business.

When Otto Frank realized that Holland would be engulfed in war he decided to turn a few ramshackle rooms at the top of his business premises into a secret hiding place. A bookcase was built in front of a small doorway leading to them. He and his wife had two daughters: Margot born in 1926, and Annelies Marie who was three years younger. When, on 5 July 1942, Margot received a summons for transportation to Germany, both the Frank family and the van Daans went into hiding in the rooms behind the bookcase. Food, magazines and books were brought to them secretly by four members of the firm and they also had a radio.

Anne was given a diary by her parents for her thirteenth birthday on 12 June 1942 and in it began to describe her life in hiding. Since the first edition of 1946 it has been translated into some 40 languages. The rooms where the Franks and van Daans hid for so many months without ever going out, are small and bare. A Jewish dentist friend, Mr Dussel, joined them. Magazine and newspaper pictures were stuck on the walls by Margot and Anne and are still there. One is of Princess Elizabeth and Princess Margaret of England, another of Deanna Durbin as a teenage movie star.

The last entry in Anne's diary was on 1 August 1944, the day that they were all betrayed to the Gestapo. It is uncertain who did this. Anne's diary went unnoticed by her German captors and was kept by one of the Franks' friends.

Van Daan died in a gas chamber; his wife's fate is unknown. Mrs Frank and the two girls were sent to Auschwitz until the Russians advanced, when they were then evacuated with other prisoners to Belsen. There, Mrs Frank died after she struck a guard who tried to assault Margot. Anne displayed great courage and endurance throughout the months of her ordeal. Then both Anne and Margot caught typhus. One ghastly day Margot, who tried to get up from her bunk which was above Anne's, fell to the floor and broke her neck. At last Anne's brave spirit was crushed. It was the final blow from which even this courageous girl could not recover and a few days later she died. Perhaps the greatest part of the tragedy is that she never knew what inspiration her diary would bring to thousands of people all over the world.

Otto Frank managed to survive and returned to Amsterdam at the end of May 1945. He was given Anne's diary and 312 pages of notes, a book of quotations and a book of stories. It had never entered his head to publish the writings of his daughter, but he did wish to have them translated for his mother, who had emigrated to Switzerland, and for other members of the family. For this reason a copy of Anne's writings was given to Werner Cahn, who in turn showed them to two well-known Dutch historians, Drs Jan and Annie Romein-Verschoor. The result was the publishing of Anne Frank's diary.

The Anne Frank House has now been turned into an international youth centre for the promotion of understanding in the spirit of the diary. Nothing can describe this better than Anne's own words:

> In spite of everything I still believe that people are really good at heart. If I look up into the heavens I think that it will all come right, that this cruelty too will end and that peace and tranquility will return again.

Our Lord in the Attic House

Many of the seventeenth-century houses in Holland have secret passages, attics, cellars and rooms with tragic stories. A happier one is that of Our Lord in the Attic. The title seems strange as one so often associates hidden Christian worship with catacombs and caves. During the Reformation there were some 23 underground or concealed churches, but this one, at 20 Voorburgwal, can still be visited today and is a gem of its kind. Hidden in a long attic over three houses it is about five minutes walk from the Central Station or the Dam. Opening hours are from 10 a.m. until 5 p.m. on weekdays and 1 a.m. till 5 p.m. on Sundays.

The houses were built in 1661 by Jan Hartman, whose son was a priest. Hartman lived in the house overlooking the canal and rented the other two. He was a rich merchant with a hosiery business. His front door gave on to a long hallway with a drawing room on the right. It is still furnished in Louis XV style and has sliding shutters. The walls are hung with portraits of famous people of the day including two of Jan Baptist van Eechhout and his wife, Johanna Francisca de Roy. He is seen with his dog, and his wife has a bird perched on her hand. Behind this room is a smaller one with a reading desk and more paintings. There is now an opening in this room which gives onto two staircases, one of which leads to the church.

There is a door on the first landing which divided the living quarters from the church. The drawing room on this floor is magnificent with such a large fireplace that you could walk into it. It is lined with blue and white Delft tiles and is made of walnut with twisted marble pillars. The frame has the family coat of arms and brass handles to grasp when you hold your feet up to warm them at the fire. A hart has pride of place in the coat of arms because of the first syllable in the merchant's name. The church upstairs was known at one time as the 'Church of the Hart' for the same reason. The large painting over the mantelpiece is entitled *The Presentation in the Temple*.

Opposite the vast chimney piece there is a walnut cupboard which could be used as a bed and is edged with pilasters topped with Corinthian capitals. The wooden ceiling is carved, painted and gilded and has an ornate brass chandelier. On the next floor there is a small bedroom with another built-in cupboard bed. It looks as if it is still used; a candle sconce hangs from the wall, a brown stone chamber pot is beneath the bed, a foot warmer is to hand and heavy curtains are there to be drawn over the wall recess.

At the top of the next flight of stairs you find yourself in the church. It is so conventional you almost forget you are in three attics. When Jan Hartman built his houses he did so with the idea of his attic church in mind. The galleries on either side of the altar have carved railings. The organ is still pumped by hand for concerts. The baroque altar has a revolving rosewood tabernacle which could be hidden. Before it there are mahogany communion rails, and above it is one of three interchangeable paintings by Jacob de Wit. The pulpit can also be stowed away behind the altar at will. Silver angels are placed before two columns flanking the altar; two more stand above the gilded acanthus leaves of the capitals and practically touch the ceiling. The congregation face the altar or sit along the sides of the galleries and at the back of the long room stand two larger-than-life statues of St Peter and St Paul by Jacob Cressant. If you look beyond the statues through great long windows you can gaze down over the canal and trees – a scene as beautiful as any stained-glass window.

Further steps lead up to a spiral staircase and then out to the galleries. From the windows up here the view is even more impressive and you can see St Nicholas' Church and the charming old roofs of Amsterdam. Behind the top of the altar there is a narrow passage to a small cell with a tiny altar.

You leave the church by going downstairs in one of the other houses, passing, on your way, another small chapel. Then comes a landing fitted with confessional boxes, some seventeenth-century paintings and glass cases of church plate. There is a map of Amsterdam on the wall. When you touch a light switch tiny bulbs come on to show you exactly where the other concealed churches were during the Reformation.

After leaving the church turn again towards the main station into New Bridge Street, a short street leading to the New Bridge which crosses a canal. Many of the boat sightseeing tours start from here. Houses edging the water seem to grow out of it and the scene is very Venetian. The Old Church tower adds to the skyline.

Two identical houses, the Silver Mirrors, overhang the roadway and have been converted into a tavern restaurant. These lovely old twin buildings, said to be two of the oldest in the city, are of red brick with wooden shutters and stepped gables. A former mayor of Amsterdam built them for his two daughters. They are exact replicas of each other to prove that he loved both his daughters equally! The interior is in old-fashioned style with copper pans and a large oak bar. The restaurant is upstairs and offers a good menu with reasonable prices.

The Western Church, Amsterdam's largest Renaissance church, is again of red brick with enormous gables. Queen Beatrix was married there. Built in 1632 it has not only the highest tower in the city but also one of the most beautiful. The golden crown on top of it was presented by Maximilian of Austria. Rembrandt's tomb is in this church.

Of the many squares in Amsterdam the Mint Square is outstanding. Seven streets converge on it and pride of place is given to the Mint Tower where coins were made long ago. As always there is a clock beneath the open belfry. Nobody staying in the city can ever claim to forget the time!

In another square off the Kalverstraat there is a little statue reminiscent of the Bad Boy of Koblenz or the 'Manneken-Pis' in Brussels. It is of a grinning boy, hands on hips, who symbolises youth.

Rembrandt's house

Rembrandt's house is close to the Montelbaanstoren (again a tower with clock) which soars high above the surrounding district and is a great favourite with painters and photographers.

The painter's house has an attractive façade with red shutters. He lived here for nearly 20 years. Yet, unhappily, before he was 40 years old, in this same house both his adored wife Saskia and his only son Titus died. It is still furnished in the same way as when he lived there. You can see many of his etchings and copper printing plates and it was here that some of his most famous works, including the enormous *Night Watch*, were painted.

Rembrandt Harmensz van Rijn was born in Leyden where his father was a miller. His family lived well and the boy was given a good education at the local Latin school. His father wanted him to enter university. However, the desire to paint had already asserted itself, and his father agreed to apprentice him for three years to the painter Jacob van Swanenbirgh. He then studied a further six months in Amsterdam with another artist, Pieter Lastman.

By the time he was 23 he was an independent portrait painter with his own pupils. From the beginning his art never lacked admirers. In his etchings he drew on copper plate with a pen of hard steel which threw up minute particles of metal on either side of the cut. When printed these gave a dark blurred pattern which enhanced the print. In his painting he became preoccupied with chiaroscuro and his play with light and shade was original and revealing. Over the years he gathered together a splendid collection of jewels, arms, oriental robes and lavish materials to use in his portraits. Meanwhile, he fell in love with Saskia, a beautiful relative of his landlord, and they married in 1634. She posed for many of his works but, despite these enchanting pictures, even in his early years Rembrandt seemed drawn towards old people as models. Although their careworn faces are skilfully highlighted and their hands done with almost painful precision, they are treated with sympathy and affection.

Of his four children only one survived, the boy Titus. During his son's infancy Rembrandt did many appealing drawings of small children and Titus sat for him so often that by them the onlooker can watch the child grow to manhood. It is curious that Rembrandt, who was always attracted by the inner spirit of his sitters, should have painted so many self-portraits. They show him in every mood and at all ages. In his last one, in senile decay, one cannot believe that this pathetic figure is the brilliant artist himself. If the portrait is true, the level of his genius had not faded with time.

After Saskia died, Titus had a nurse until he was eight years old. From that time a young servant, Hendrickje Stoffels, looked after him and managed the household. She became Rembrandt's mistress, but whether she eventually married him or not is not known although she bore him a daughter, Cornelia. Rembrandt had extravagant tastes and, although famous and receiving large fees for his work, he was careless and became increasingly indifferent about money. His debts mounted with the years. When Hendrickje died his creditors brought more pressure to bear on him. Titus eventually came into money from Saskia's estate which alleviated the situation temporarily. He then married the daughter of a silversmith, Magdalena van Loo, but, in less than a year, he too died and the ageing Rembrandt did not survive the loss of his only son for more than a few months.

Whatever sorrow his private life brought, his powerful technique never left him. His marvellous portraits with their sentiment and realism brought a depth to painting which the world still acclaims.

The Waag or Weighing House

Most of Amsterdam's beautiful buildings were designed during the seventeenth century, Holland's Golden Age, but in Neumarkt Square you will find an older, fifteenth-century building, called the Waag or Weighing House, at one time used for weighing merchandise. It looks like a medieval turreted castle but was converted from a circular gatehouse in the town battlements. It became a guildhouse during Rembrandt's time and the city's surgeons' guild gave weekly lessons there. Rembrandt painted two of his most famous works within its walls, both of them anatomy lessons. The Waag has been turned into a museum for old prints and drawings of Amsterdam.

Rijksmuseum

No visit to Holland would be complete without going to the Rijksmuseum. Here you will find more Rembrandt paintings than anywhere else (except the Mauritshuis), including the *Night Watch*, which nearly covers a complete wall in one gallery. The building, castle-like with its towers, was designed by P. J. H. Cuypers in the Dutch Renaissance style. The exterior is embellished with sculptures and tile work and it is surrounded by parkland. The gardens are a favourite background for wedding photographs.

The museum is a treasure trove with paintings by Jan Steen, Johannes Vermeer, Pieter de Hooch, Franz Hals and many others of the Flemish and Dutch schools, as well as the works of Rubens, Veronese, Tintoretto and Goya. It is open during the week from 10 a.m. until 5 p.m. and on Sundays from 1 a.m. till 5 p.m. and closed on Mondays. On the ground floor there are general antiquities such as eighteenth-century glassware and tiny medieval dolls' houses in high cabinets which you can reach by step ladders. There is also a very good restaurant and souvenir gallery.

The rooms on the first floor are carefully arranged and start with Flemish religious paintings of the 1500s. One that brings a smile is the *Egg Dance* by Pieter Aertsz where merrymakers are dancing but must avoid breaking eggs placed strategically on the floor. Another by Pieter Saenredan reveals how the Dam looked in 1597. Two portraits by Franz Hals, one of a smiling old lady, show how he conveys the impression of lace ruffles with a few brush strokes. Hals, as a portrait painter regarded second only to Rembrandt in Holland, was the pioneer of free broad brush work, a technique completely different from Rembrandt's.

The other prominent portraits by Hals are of an attractive young couple in Dutch costume standing in an Italian garden enjoying a joke together, and the famous *Jolly Toper* who holds his glass out to the onlooker with a generous smile on his bleary face. Hals knew only too well how his sitter felt, for he himself was an alcoholic.

The gallery walls in the first series of rooms are white, the paintings hung singly. More often than not this applies to the rest of the building, and is effective when one remembers other museums with pictures clustered together due to lack of space.

In a small ante-room tiny paintings are displayed on rust-coloured velvet, lit from above. These range from miniatures to small pictures about 6 or 7 in (15 or 17.5 cm) high. Four of the latter, charmingly painted by Van Deverne, represent the four seasons.

Each room seems to have more beautiful paintings than the last. There are pictures by Avercamp and Steen. Avercamp's *Ice Scene* has so much detail that it is hard to tear yourself away from it. A river has frozen up near village houses, and both young and old are enjoying displaying their versatility in the sunshine. Skaters weave in and out between horse-drawn sleighs, row boats are squeezed up by the frost, people play hockey and couples dance together. Some children are learning to skate, one has fallen down, dogs frisk about and bark, and birds from nearby trees fly overhead and add to the activity.

Jan Steen's *Feast of St Nicholas* is equally fascinating. Everyone is overjoyed with the gifts the Saint has brought except one small boy. His mother is comforting him and explaining that his present will arrive at any moment. A small girl holds her new dolls' house close to her, reluctant to give it to her grandmother for even a few moments, although the old lady is holding out her hands for it.

Titus as a Monk is the title of Rembrandt's portrait of his son in a monk's hooded robe. The cowl is softly draped about the face and the youth is in contemplative mood. Rembrandt's *Stone Bridge,* one of his few landscapes, shows flat countryside and a threatening sky. A portrait of his mother always attracts people. She sits in a pool of light from a window, reading her bible and following the words slowly by tracing them with her fingers. His *Bridal Couple* may be a portrait of Titus and his wife at the time of their marriage. It is also known as *The Jewish Bride* and again sometimes as *Ruth and Boaz.* This sensitive painting shows a young man holding his hand over his bride's heart to feel it beating. Their costly clothes are in golds and reds, the girl's jewels lavish and she wears a string of irridescent pearls round her neck.

Rembrandt's *Anatomy Lecture of Dr John Deyman* is part of a larger painting which was damaged. It has the same background as his *Anatomy Lecture of Dr Nicholas Tulp* at the Mauritshuis in The Hague. Both were done in the Waag in the Guild of Surgeons small operating theatre.

The famous *Night Watch* is beautifully displayed in its own gallery. In the centre of the gallery there is a rectangular table with vases of fresh flowers seemingly arranged just before you enter, and there are seats to rest and admire the magnificent painting. When it was cleaned in 1947 and layers of dark varnish removed it was found to be a daytime scene, not one of night. The colours glow, and lively figures look as if they might walk out of the canvas at any moment. The splendidly dressed men represent a number of musketeers, led by Frans Banning Cocq, who were part of the Civic Guard of Amsterdam. Nobody remains unmoved by the virility of this masterpiece. The next Rembrandt, *The Sampling Officials of the Drapers' Guild,* also shows genius in the subtle way the sunlight filters through a window to light up the white collars on the black robes of the guild members.

Gallery follows gallery. You will see Pieter de Hooch's domestic scenes, noted for their charm and warm human feeling. *The Linen Press* shows crisp linen being proudly put away. A subject not particularly dear to anyone's heart is of a mother searching her child's head for lice.

The Vermeers must not be missed. His *Kitchen Maid* is of a sturdy girl in a yellow bodice holding a pitcher and pouring milk into a bowl. Behind her on the floor a little foot warmer glows. His scene of Delft, *The Little Street,* transports one back to that bewitching, quiet town. Probably his most captivating picture is *Young Woman Reading a Letter.* Her expression does not betray her feelings. The deep blue velour upholstery of the chairs and light blue walls serve to emphasize the pale blue of her smock. She is pregnant.

Opposite the Rijksmuseum, across the canal, is the Nieuwe Spiegelstraat – Mirror Street – where an exploratory stroll often pays dividends, for it is full of antique shops where you can buy almost anything from old furniture to new statuettes. Wares overflow from the shops onto the pavements and on sunny days there is a smell of wax polish and the musty odour of old books.

Vincent van Gogh Museum

Just a few minutes walk from the Rijksmuseum, in Paulus Potterstraat, is the Vincent van Gogh Museum, a stark modern building in complete contrast to its neighbour. Here you will find the world's most complete collection (more than 200) of this artist's works, letters and mementos. There are about 150 of his familiar paintings such as the *Potato Eaters* and *Portrait of my room at Arles.* Of the latter he wrote to Gauguin:

> I enjoyed immensely doing this plain interior; it is as simple as a Seurat; the tones crudely brushed on and with a heavy impasto; the walls pale lilac, the floor a faded broken red, the chairs and bed lemony green. I wanted to express a feeling of perfect rest, you see, by means of all the various tones among which there is no white at all except for a small note within the black frame of the mirror.

Van Gogh painted a whole series of sunflower pictures and here you will see his most famous one, *Sunflowers, Arles 1888.* To him these flowers always seemed a symbol of the sun, with which he had an obsession. Even on a grey day the painting shines with its symphony of yellows, the flowers in full bloom. He was to write: 'The flowers fade so soon and the thing is to do the whole thing in a rush'.

Van Gogh spent the first five years of his life as an artist in Holland. He worked furiously, but was under emotional strain during this time. He quarrelled with his parents and had a disastrous love affair. Things were no better for him when he later set up home with a prostitute in The Hague. His paintings of peasants at work culminated in the masterpiece the *Potato Eaters*, not in the radiant colours he was to use later, but in sombre tones of green, black and brown.

In 1886 he moved to Paris where he met Toulouse-Lautrec and Emile Bernard. Later he became friends with Gauguin, and was further inspired by the great works of the older Impressionists such as Degas, Monet and Pissarro.

The museum has daylight excluded from one floor for his drawings and collection of Japanese prints. In other galleries you will see works by Gauguin, Laval, Monticelli and other artists of the period. The sales desk has reproductions and books. There is a library and reading room (open on weekdays) for those who wish to learn more about van Gogh. Unfortunately, mentally unbalanced and often in the depths of despair, this incredibly gifted artist shot himself on 27 July 1890 and died two days later at the early age of 37.

The Rijksmuseum, the van Gogh and the Stedelijk are all close together in Amsterdam and the Vondel Park is also near.

Stedelijk Museum

Like the Vincent van Gogh Museum the Stedelijk Municipal Museum is in Paulus Potterstraat. The permanent collection from 1850 is augmented by modern and contemporary art exhibitions by famous Dutch and international artists such as Karl Appel, Willem de Koonig, Chagal, Calder Oldenburg and Segal. The souvenir shop has a wide selection of reproductions, colour slides and postcards. The restaurant opens into a charming sculpture garden.

Even closer to the Stedelijk than the Rijksmuseum is the Concertgebouw at the end of Museumplein. It was built in 1888 and has two auditoriums, one for recitals and chamber music and the other for orchestral concerts. The Concertgebouw Orchestra has 116 members and gives 133 concerts a year.

There are some 40 other museums to visit, amongst them the Tropical Museum which has a special Africa Hall, an Islamic Hall and many strange curiosities from the tropics. A Tobacco Museum is unusual with porcelain, clay and wooden pipes. There is a Madame Tussauds wax museum, a branch of the famous London one, with figures of international politicians, film stars and famous people past and present, including a tableau of Rembrandt in his studio.

Maritime Museum

The views from this building, the original arsenal of the Amsterdam Admiralty (built in 1656), overlook water to the east of the main railway station. The official opening took place in 1981 and the exhibition gives an overall picture of the Dutch at sea. The major themes – commerce, fisheries, war, yachting and navigation – are represented by ship models, paintings, charts, instruments and weapons. There is a State Barge in ivory and gold (built in 1816 and over 50 ft [15 m] long) which was used on ceremonial occasions until 1962. From its gilded prow Neptune drives his team of seahorses. Three historical ships are moored at the landing stage outside.

Windmills and parks

For those not interested in museums there are seven picturesque windmills preserved in Amsterdam, two of which, 'De Gooyer' and 'Bloem', are still used to grind corn. These are included in several of the excursions organized by the VVV.

The city's most popular park is close by Museumplein and is named after one of Holland's best known poets of the past, Joost van den Vondel. Its pathways are a favourite place for strollers, joggers and people walking their dogs but, as it covers 120 acres (49 ha), there is plenty of space. Weeping willows sweep the grass, and amongst the ponds is an impressive automated fountain in a stream which goes through a cycle of different patterns. Being Holland there are flower beds everywhere.

Shopping

Besides the shopping streets and stores already mentioned Amsterdam is well known for its open-air street markets and you will find one somewhere almost every day of the week. Tourists enjoy the general market in Albert Cuypstraat, just beyond the Heineken Brewery. It is where local housewives go for vegetables, fruit and general produce, and visitors can find Dutch cheese, wooden clogs and other souvenirs. Smaller streets criss-crossing the canals contain a surprising number of shops selling glass, china, woollens, teas and spices and, of course, Delft ware.

Should you ponder what to do in the evening a quick glance through the weekly magazine *Amsterdam This Week* will give you some ideas, for there is a wide choice of plays and films. Every week of the year, summer as well as winter, there are concerts and recitals at the Concertgebouw, musicals and operettas at the Carre, ballet or dance at the

Stadschouwburg, organ recitals in historic churches, and English language plays in up to a score of theatres throughout the city. In addition, there is the wide ranging programme of the annual Holland Festival every June.

Amstel Hotel

Probably the most prestigious and certainly the best-loved hotel in Amsterdam is the Amstel. As its name implies its elegant setting is on the banks of the river Amstel. It was designed and built by a Dr Sarphati and opened in 1867 – more than a decade before the Krasnapolsky. A traditional palatial hotel of that era it was immediately patronized by royalty and cosmopolitan society, but many rooms remained empty.

When it was first decided to build the hotel an open letter was sent to the mayor of Amsterdam stating that the project was too extravagant and that a small city (as Amsterdam then was) did not warrant a luxury hotel. Despite opposition the hotel was built, and initially ran at a loss. However, as news of it travelled, more guests came and, eventually, success was assured by the arrival in 1870 of Dr John Mezger who became a resident. He was the founder in the Netherlands of medical gymnastics and massage. His fame soon reached European royalty and nobility. For weeks, sometimes months, they came to stay at the Amstel for a cure. Scattered throughout the VIP guest book are the names of the Empress Eugenie, wife of Napoleon III, the Empress Elizabeth of Austria, wife of Franz Joseph, the Kings of Belgium, Sweden, Saxony and Bulgaria, The Grand Dukes Nicholas, Vladimir and Sergius of Russia, and the King of Siam.

Business at the hotel was so good it was decided to enlarge it and put in extra bathrooms to attract more foreigners. In 1907 a journal describes the entrance hall as being magnificent, especially at night when guests were in evening clothes and uniforms. The rustle of the ladies' taffeta and silken frocks as they descended the wide double staircase added to the glamour already created by the soft lights. Crystal flowers topped the balustrade pillars and added to the glitter cast by an enormous chandelier.

The suites today are beautifully designed, the bathrooms carrying on the motifs of the drawing rooms and bedrooms. When Queen Juliana and Prince Bernard celebrated their silver wedding anniversary they invited the royal couples who attended to stay at the Amstel, including Queen Elizabeth and Prince Philip, the Shah of Iran and his Empress and the King and Queen of Thailand. When Queen Beatrix was married her wedding reception was held at the Amstel.

Recently the hotel has been refurbished and the meeting rooms now have full audio visual and simultaneous translation facilities. Its superb restaurant, La Rive, shares a river terrace with the bar which is open every night until 1 a.m. for drinks and light refreshments. The hotel is famous for its Sunday champagne brunch buffet held in the Spiegelzaal. In addition, it can provide a luxury canal boat, with buffet and bar, capable of taking up to 50 guests on a romantic Amsterdam cruise.

Amsterdam Hilton

The Amsterdam Hilton could not be more conveniently situated for the visiting motorist. Being in a residential area, 138-140 Apollolaan, it has its own car park with capacity for 200 cars, unusual in crowded Amsterdam. Its frontage is so extravagantly landscaped with flower beds full of blossoms that no earth can be seen. At the back of the hotel a terrace restaurant and café overlook a wide canal, yet the hotel is within walking distance of the famous Concertgebouw, the Stedelijk, van Gogh and Rijksmuseums. The RAI conference centre and World Trade Centre are not far away.

The Hilton Kei restaurant offers authentic Japanese food including Sashi and Tappen-Yaki. It has a view out over the canal, as does the Half Moon bar. The latter is named after the vessel *De Halve Maan* which took Henry Hudson, the English navigator, to the shores of the New World in search of a north-west or north-east passage to China and Japan. The bar is a well-known meeting place for guests and locals alike and during winter there is the welcoming warmth of an open fire.

Amsterdam Apollo Hotel

Close to the Amsterdam Hilton and also in Apollolaan, at No. 5, is the Apollo Hotel, a five-star international hotel belonging to the Trusthouse Forte chain. Again motorists can note that it has its own parking facilities and it faces one of the tree-lined avenues of Amsterdam.

The hotel gets its name, like the avenue it faces, from a nearby bodega which was built next to a stadium erected for the Olympic games in 1928. Eventually the bodega became a cinema, but new plans are in hand by Trusthouse Forte to incorporate it into the hotel as a health and sports centre. There are eight luxurious suites as well as 220 rooms. Other amenities include boutiques, a hairdressing salon, a waterside terrace bar and restaurant. It has its own Brown Café, aptly named the Bodega, which has a quiet, old fashioned atmosphere with dark walls, shelves near the ceiling clustered with hanging plants and old bottles. Windows overlook the canals to give a mobile panorama.

Hôtel de l'Europe

The Hotel de l'Europe, 2 Nieuwe Doelenstraat, is another hotel which seeks to pamper its guests. Its situation near the Mint Square, where the Amstel river meets Rokin, means that many bedrooms overlook the river. The cuisine is well known and its restaurant is rated highly by the *Guide Michelin*. It offers a choice of more than 50 tasty *hors d'oeuvres* and is famed for its wild boar ham.

Hotel Pulitzer

This hotel in Prinsengracht 315-331 is certainly out of the ordinary for several reasons. A company headed by an American, Peter Pulitzer, renovated and linked together several canalside houses and buildings to make it. They cleverly left the gardens where they were so that guests often leave a public room to find themselves in an outdoor café or flower garden. It was a brilliant idea, for some of the buildings were private houses, others warehouses, one once belonged to the East India Company and some date back to the early 1600s. The result is charming and different, and outside the neck spouts, clock gables and façades have been painstakingly restored.

Across a canal from the hotel lies Amsterdam's old Jordaan district, a sort of Greenwich Village, Montmartre and East End rolled into one. Its inhabitants, as you might expect, are a mixture of artists, writers, families who have lived there for generations and students who can still afford the ever-rising rents. There is plenty of atmosphere, for its tiny streets are filled with cafés, shops, boutiques and bars. It is a mecca for visitors especially at weekends when the traffic is less busy.

There is a story that when a tourist couple booked in at the Pulitzer they settled into their room for a wash, unpacked and then decided to explore Amsterdam for a while before dinner. On the way back to the hotel they felt weary and stopped to have a meal at the first nice restaurant they saw. It was a delightful French one and they had an excellent meal. Feeling refreshed they ordered a taxi to return to their hotel. The waiter called one and asked where they wanted to go. 'The Pulitzer' said the man, whereupon both waiter and driver started to laugh. Sensing that the man was irritated the waiter controlled himself and said 'Forgive us laughing, Sir, but you see you are at the Pulitzer. This is our French restaurant. It faces the street.' The confusion was understandable because the De Goudesbloem, as it is called, is located between a bar and the coffee shop. There is also a separate entrance at 8 Reestraat through what was at one time a pharmacy.

Each year the Pulitzer sponsors a series of concerts and recitals in its salons and gardens and an annual canal concert on barges moored opposite the main entrance.

Amsterdam Sonesta

The Amsterdam Sonesta is on the banks of one of the city's oldest canals, the Singel, with its own pier for glass-topped sightseeing boats. Like the Pulitzer it started as 13 medieval houses linked by an underground tunnel with a seventeenth-century Lutheran church. The latter was built between 1668 and 1671 by wealthy Lutheran burghers and has an interesting background.

Amsterdammers named it Koepelkerk (Dome Church). Copper was ordered from Sweden for the dome and King Karel XI generously sent it free of tax. The silhouette has dominated the skyline along the Singel ever since.

In 1822 a great fire destroyed the church interior, but this was gradually restored during the next six years. It continued to be used by Lutheran parishioners until 1935, when it was deconsecrated due to the diminishing congregation. The copper dome was replaced *c*.1950 but damage had badly affected the wooden panels beneath the old one and many of them had mysteriously disappeared during the Second World War. A magnificent organ had been installed to complement the excellent acoustics and it was last used in a religious context in 1961 for the traditional *St Matthew Passion*. The impressive interior fell into an even worse state of repair, and so it remained until the Sonesta hotel planners in 1974 applied for permission to build in its vicinity and take over the church itself. It was completely renovated inside and out, even the panelled woodwork being replaced. It is now used for receptions, musical and theatrical performances and conventions.

The Sonesta has a speciality beef restaurant, the Rib Room, and an authentic Dutch pub, the Koepel Cafe. A combination of the old and the new, it has 116 rooms.

Adjacent to the Sonesta is the Holland Art and Craft Centre where revived ancient skills are demonstrated. There are cigar makers, wool spinners, stained-glass artisans, potters, silversmiths, painters, pewter casters and many other craftsmen. Artists paint original Delft blue china and clog makers ply their trade. It is an ideal place to buy Dutch gifts.

De Gouden Kettingh Hotel

One of the pleasant reasons for visiting Holland is that there are plenty of spotlessly clean small hotels at modest prices. De Gouden Kettingh is one of these, close to the Pulitzer, near the city centre and overlooking the inevitable canal. The bathrooms only have showers but your breakfast will be as delicious as at any *de luxe* hotel. The name means 'The Golden Necklace', and there is a story connected with it.

In 1650 the original house was built by a merchant. In 1653 he and his family went away on holiday. When they returned home his wife discovered that a golden necklace was missing. Suspicion fell on a housemaid and she was arrested by the police and taken to the Town Hall in Dam Square for questioning. She confessed her guilt on the rack and was hanged in public in the square without revealing what had happened to the necklace. A few years later, when the roof of the house was being repaired, it was found hidden under the tiles. The merchant's wife hung it on the wall outside her house as the final evidence of the maid's guilt.

In 1981 the house was joined to the one next door and the present small hotel is the result. It has 18 rooms.

Brown Cafés

Brown Cafés (*kroegjes*) are the traditional neighbourhood cafés and bars found all over the city. They are often centuries old and decorated in sombre colours – hence their name – but there is nothing dull about the atmosphere for they are lively friendly places. Here are the names of a few. The Café Kalkhoven, dating back to 1670 is in Prinsengracht, as are Papaneiland at No. 2, De Prins at No. 124 and De Eland at No. 296. Café Chris is at 42 Bloemstraat and Bols Taverne at 106 Rozengracht. Wynand Fockink at 31 Pijlsteeg, just behind the Dam Square, is one of the city's most historic. Dimly lit, its walls are lined with shelves holding dozens of strange, handpainted bottles from the past.

For the casual visitor nothing is more fascinating than the core of Amsterdam with its high steeples and tower clocks, the bright flower stalls, the endless streams of cyclists and the herring vendors. What could be more attractive than the lines of the glorious seventeenth-century architecture, cobbled streets, bridges and the leisurely flowing canals? Or the muted colours of the leaning buildings with their characteristic stepped gables, the floating flower market at Singel, the carillon concerts, the glass-topped boats and the canal illuminations hanging just above the water after sunset?

3

EXCURSIONS FROM AMSTERDAM

Broek, Monnikendam, Volendam, Marken and Edam

Broek

Amsterdam can be the starting point for many excursions. Broek (the word means trousers in Dutch) in Waterland is a mere 7 miles (11 km) distant and can easily be reached after going through the Ij tunnel beneath the harbour. It is a minute village and is far nicer out of season as the roads are narrow and there are often places where cars cannot pass each other. It grew up around a small harbour. Each tiny white-painted house has a handkerchief-size garden, white shutters, and behind the windows flowers cover the glass and pots are placed in gleaming copper bowls. Boats bob up and down in the harbour and ducks swim in and out of a small house built for them on an island, the house decorated with red and white diamond shapes. The one small bridge has a white balustrade and the village hall has a swan painted on it. Weeping willows hang over the roadway and add to the pretty scene. The local industry is the making of Edam cheese.

Monnikendam

From the village you motor to Monnikendam and in no time see its church steeple coming into sight. There is also the tower of the Town Hall. Watch the clock in the latter if it is near the hour because at that time small mechanical knights march around in procession. It is a colourful Town Hall, with green snakes with red tails on the balustrade. The old café, called the 'Post Horn', is one of the places where Napoleon really slept! A line of small gabled houses leads to the harbour, and, near the water's edge there is a café called the 'Stuttenburgh' which not only serves excellent tea but has all kinds of musical boxes. If, when you walk around the quaint streets, you notice a tangy smell it is because Monnikendam is famous for its eel smoking.

Volendam

After following the main highway once more and crossing an inlet of the Ijselmeer, you ride along the top of a sea dyke to Volendam. Although Volendam is primarily a fishing village, the people make much of their living from tourism. They are used to being photographed and even the children will pose readily. Roman Catholicism thrives here and the people are very inbred. The idea of marrying someone from nearby Marken, which is Protestant, would never enter anybody's head, and vice versa.

The villagers wear their regional dress, which is colourful and attractive. For special occasions the women and children have seven-coloured striped skirts in red, white, black, green, yellow and two shades of blue, with an edging of red and white cord along the bottom. The skirts are kept in their bell shape by two starched petticoats worn beneath. The caps are of stiff white lace with a wing out to each side. A triple necklace of coral beads hangs round the neck with a golden clasp at the back. Sometimes spotted muslin fichus are worn over the flowered chintz bodices.

The men have wide baggy trousers, fitted black jackets with blue facings, and tall black hats. Their coats are fastened with two half-guilder pieces and their cuff buttons are silver.

13 *Hanging clothes without pegs*

When you drive into Volendam along the Ijselmeer all the little houses are pointed and, save for the different flower arrangements in the windows, all look alike. Suddenly you come upon the harbour and continue along the dyke with the water to the right and a line of houses on the left. A statue of the Virgin Mary stands at the head of the harbour. Souvenir shops mingle with the houses along the waterfront and, if it happens to be washday, you will see lines of unpegged clothes along the dyke edge, but miraculously nothing blows away. The women twist two ropes together to make their clothes lines so that they can trap things between them and do not need pegs to secure them.

The brownish fishing boats have black sails and there are still a few old *botters* left which are purely local. These single-masted boats are high in the prow, broad of beam and were developed in olden times when the Zuyder Zee opened into the North Sea.

Marken

Over the water lies the flat green island of Marken. It is less than 1 mile (1.5 km) wide, and 2 miles (3 km) long and is reached by a 2 mile (3 km) causeway. The costumes of these island people have been influenced by

14 *Traditional costume at Marken*

the Orient. The children dress alike until they are six years old, so that it is difficult to tell the difference between boys and girls. Both have ringlets, but the boys wear blue skirts. Different types of clothes are worn for special occasions: for summer, winter, Whitsun, weddings, mournings and so on. Some of the lovely costumes are over 100 years old. A bridegroom wears a top hat and has a black waistcoat braided with red and yellow. There are 32 silver buttons down the front and a silver wedding chain is worn around the neck.

Marken house interiors are most attractive. The fireplaces and chimneys up to the ceilings are lined with Delft tiles. Clothes and linen are kept in ornate chests hand-painted with roses and tulips. Inside the church it is surprising to see a barque and a herring boat suspended from the ceiling. They are to remind parishioners of their fishing heritage. The people of Marken are Calvinists with a rigid way of life. Shops and any place of entertainment are closed on Sundays. There are lots of little shops and a small harbour.

Edam

Carrying on from Volendam you come, almost immediately, to the little village of Edam. It gave birth to the famous Edam cheese, now widely imitated. This practice of imitation became so widespread that in 1952 countries outside Holland were barred from making imitations by the

15 *The Town Hall, dating from 1737, at Edam*

International Cheese Conventions of Strasbourg.

A broad canal runs parallel to the main street, which is a charming place to walk, for all Edam's buildings are here. Many of them date back to the sixteenth century, while the church was built in 1475. Its carillon is one of the oldest in the country and the chimes were cast in 1561. The Weighing Hall for cheeses is unusual, with hand-painted scenes on its façade, and the Town Hall has a green and gilt council chamber which is regarded as one of the finest of its kind in Holland.

An amusing story is told of a one-time mayor of Edam, Pieter Dirksz, who grew a red beard so long that it had to be folded over his arm while he was walking. When he leaned over the canal bridge near the Town Hall his beard hung over the water below. When the tip grew moist the villagers knew the tide was in!

Edam cheeses are sold with great ceremony in nearby Alkmaar every Friday morning. They arrive by barge and passers-by watch as the round cheeses, small and large, are thrown ashore to the waiting porters. When they are brought to the market square, hung with international flags on market day, the buyers cluster round to examine them. They appear to stand about just clapping their hands, but this is the traditional way in which they have bought for centuries. Bidders clap each others' hands while shouting prices. A final hand clasp clinches the deal. The price is then entered on a board for all to see.

Once the prices are settled the porters, or to give them their official title, the Guild of Cheese Carriers, again take over. They are a great tourist draw because of their festive dress. They wear white suits and belong to four different companies. Coloured straw hats in red, green, blue or yellow denote their employer. The hats are shaped a little like those worn by gondoliers and have streamers down the back. These men pile cheeses – there are two kinds: round Edams and wheel-shaped Goudas – on flat-bottomed wooden floats. These have curved shafts like sledge runners, again in company colours, and are hoisted off the ground and suspended from hooks on harnesses which the men wear over their shoulders. The cheeses are carried to the weighhouse to be placed on scales for the buyer and marked. It is always understood that the youngest and oldest porter work together, and two men between them carry 80 cheeses weighing about 350 lb (159 kg). It is a very colourful procedure and the bright yellow cheeses with their rounded shapes add to the scene. It is not until shipped abroad that the Edams are covered with their protective rind of red wax.

Hoorn and Enkhuizen
Hoorn
Hoorn is some 13 miles (20 km) from Edam, if you follow straight along

16 *The cheese market at Alkmaar*

the sea dyke. It was the home of Willems Cornelis Schouten, who was born there in 1580. A great sailor, he was the first to round the southern tip of South America, which he named Cape Hoorn after his birth place (later known internationally as Cape Horn). Another famous man born there was the explorer Jan Pieterszoon Coen, who was seven years younger. He founded Batavia, now known at Jakarta. He governed the island until his death and helped establish Holland's hold on the East Indies. Another intrepid inhabitant of Hoorn, Janszoon Tasman, circumnavigated Australia and discovered New Zealand. The island of Tasmania was named after him.

Walking around Hoorn you can visualize why the port was so important in olden times. If further proof was needed the Westfries Museum, set up in an old council house which dates from 1632, gives the right atmosphere. It has a large collection of art treasures including instruments, etchings and paintings from the West Friesian past. The old Dutch market is very picturesque.

17 *The town of Hoorn*

Enkhuizen
In the neighbouring fishing port of Enkhuizen, stronghold of the former
Zuyder Zee, there is one of Holland's largest outdoor museums. Whilst
walking through it you will be able to see how people lived and worked
before the Barrier Dam (Afsluitdijk) was built. Among other things
there are fish curing sheds, a sail loft, a tannery and a steam laundry.
Altogether there are 130 authentic houses to visit, built alongside little
streets, canals and alleyways, to give you an idea of everyday life between
1880 and 1932.

The town itself is picturesque, with a stately Town Hall and old merchant houses. Former warehouses of the East Indies Corporation dating from 1620 have been converted into a large indoor museum where there are model ships and costumes and a dozen old sailing vessels.

Aalsmeer

The world's largest flower auction is held every morning except Saturday and Sunday at Aalsmeer near Schiphol airport. Get there early for the most spectacular part of the show. There are over 4000 growers of flowers and plants who are the joint owners of the auction building. Due to the ever-increasing volume of business to be handled the place now covers an area equivalent to 60 football pitches.

There are plants and flowers throughout the year, as many in winter as in summer. Although the beautiful bulb fields draw thousands of tourists each spring, 90 per cent of Dutch flowers are nowadays grown in glasshouses. Computerized indicators in the auction halls keep track of the sales, and traders can collect their merchandise within 15 minutes of auctioning. In many cases aircraft cargo containers on trailers are filled in the building and driven straight to the airport, so that the goods can be anywhere in the world by the same evening or the following morning. There are extensive catwalk galleries above the sales floors connecting the auction rooms, and tourists can walk along these and look down on the colourful proceedings.

Haarlem

It is easy to reach Haarlem from Amsterdam. The town, capital of the province of North Holland, is a bare 15 miles (24 km) west along a four-lane motorway. In earlier times people left Amsterdam by track boat from the Haarlem Gate and entered the city of Haarlem via the Amsterdam Gate. In 1839 the first steam train, the *Arend,* carried passengers between the two cities. Today it is a mere 20-minute commuter ride. The two cities have grown closer together as their modern residential areas have extended towards one another. Once in Haarlem everything is within a radius of 6 miles (10 km): the sea with its beaches; forests; lakes; *polders,* and historic buildings. Most exciting for flower lovers, Haarlem is the nerve centre of the bulb industry.

The main attraction in the town is the Grote Markt, one of Holland's most splendid squares, with a variety of architecture and a fine statue of Laurens Koster, the inventor of printing. It was in the ancient Knight's Hall, now part of the Town Hall, that William II granted Haarlem its city rights. It was rebuilt at the beginning of the seventeenth century, although many thirteenth-century beams remain from the time it was a palace of the Counts of Holland. Among its collection of antiquities there are some lovely goblets, and its small picture gallery boasts several Frans Hals portraits.

The meat market is suitably decorated on its high gables with oxen and sheep heads and, despite its original trade, is a most impressive Renaissance building which today houses the city's archives.

The gem of the square is the beautiful Gothic church of St Bavo. Its great height and the steepness of its vaulted roof of cedar wood, added to its length of 460 ft (140 m), dwarf the visitor. The choir stalls and screens are delicately carved, and there are some charming models of ships presented by the Dutch-Swedish Trading Company. It has the distinction of housing one of the finest church organs in existence with four keyboards, 64 registers and 5000 pipes. Both Handel and Mozart admired it. It is used for international competitions and organ recitals. Concerts are given every Tuesday evening from 8 to 9 p.m. from 5 April into October and, in addition, every Thursday afternoon from 3 until 4 p.m. from May to October. In winter these concerts are continued about once a month.

Haarlem has many well-preserved alms houses – *hofjes* – but one for old men, close by St Bavo, became an orphanage and then, later, the famous Frans Hals museum. The city council bought it in 1906, renovated it, replaced two old wings to fit in with the style of the main façade, preserved the inner court and laid out a seventeenth-century style garden. One of the corridors is completely tiled in blue and white marble. There are more than 20 of Hals' works here. One of the most remarkable is his painting of Haarlem's Grote Markt, which looks the same as it does today, except that the people wear seventeenth-century costume and there are no cars.

Frans Hals

Frans Hals, one of the greatest portrait painters of all time, had an unorthodox and unhappy life because he was an alcoholic. It was probably due to this weakness that he so ill-treated his first wife, Anneke Hermansz, that she died prematurely. His partiality for drink enabled him to mix with tramps and drunkards and, although he was a member of the Chamber of Rhetoric and chairman of the Painters' Corporation of Haarlem, he gradually went downhill and fell into debt. His second wife did not seem able to reform him, but he managed to support her and ten children for some years until he was forced to sell even his household effects to pay a baker to whom he was indebted. In 1664 he was in such desperate straits that the municipality paid his rent and gave him an annuity of 200 florins.

Hals' subjects range from gentlemen in silk suits to fishwives, itinerant players and taverners. An unusual way to enjoy his art, during spring and summer, is to visit the gallery in the evening when you can see the paintings by candlelight.

A famous tale

Surely the first thing we hear as children about Holland is of the little boy, Pieter, who knelt all through one rainy night with his finger stuck in a hole in a dyke in order to save the *polder* and thereby the town of Haarlem, from flooding. What we were not told is that this charming story was written in 1906 by an American authoress, Mary Mapes Dodge, in a children's book of stories called *Hans Brinker and the Silver Skates*.

The eight year old Pieter, on his way home from spending an afternoon with a blind man to whom he had taken some cakes, was horrified to notice water trickling through a small hole in the dyke. He climbed up to see what he could do and put his finger in the hole to stop the flow. His shouts for help went unheard until next morning when a clergyman passed the spot and asked him what he was doing. 'I am keeping the water from running in' replied the shivering Pieter. 'Tell them to come quickly.' Help soon arrived and young Pieter was a hero. The story seems to be known by everyone, Dutch and foreigners alike. The municipality of Haarlem eventually agreed to erect a statue to Pieter at Spaarndam, on the outskirts of the town, and it was unveiled by Princess Margriet in 1950. It is of the small boy kneeling with his finger in the hole in the dyke and looking over his shoulder for help. The little figure is as beloved as the one of Peter Pan in Kensington Gardens.

Haarlem's soil is a mixture of clay and sand, which is excellent for bulbs. They are protected during the winter months by thick carpets of straw, but with spring they come to full bloom and attract people from all over the world. From mid-March to mid-May it is like carnival time. Cars, local and foreign, are wreathed with flower garlands. Street lamps are festooned with flower arrangements and baskets of blooms hang from inns and shops. Flower pictures made up of cupped tulip-heads grace lawns in front of houses whose windows are ablaze with more blossoms. Floats of all kinds with fantastic designs in flower-heads parade the streets. Haarlem and the whole countryside around it are drenched in colour.

Keukenhof

Driving through the bulb fields beyond Haarlem to Lisse and on to Keukenhof is a wonderful experience in springtime. Strips and squares of vivid red, yellow, pink, white, purple and other colours take the place of green fields and meadows. There is no noise of farm machinery because the whole bulb industry is carried on by hand, and the only movement is of bent figures tidying, weeding, spraying or picking. Flowers are everywhere – even the barges on the canals are full of them – and when there are hyacinths and narcissi the air is fragrant.

At last you come to Keukenhof, 20 miles (32 km) from Amsterdam, known variously as 'the First Wonder of Holland', 'the Flower Lover's Paradise' or 'the Spring Wonderland'. Many years ago Keukenhof was the kitchen garden of a vast estate belonging to the Countess Jacqueline of Bavaria. A replica of her castle can still be visited. The kitchen garden is now the setting each year for a springtime flower festival. Visitors arrive by the hundreds to admire ten million glowing tulips, daffodils and hyacinths in full bloom. They flower at different times roughly like this:

Tulips	10 April	to 15 May
Daffodils	end of March	to 25 April
Hyacinths	15 April	to end of April

Some 85 of the leading Dutch growers display their flowers in separate gardens arranged like a patchwork quilt in Keukenhof's 60 acre (24 ha)

18 *A farm in a bulb area*

park, which is open daily from the end of March to about mid-May from 8 a.m. to half an hour after sunset. It can easily be reached by bus from The Hague, Leiden or Haarlem, departing in each place from outside the railway station. At most stations, too, it is possible to buy a combined travel and entry ticket. For those using their own cars, all roads leading to Keukenhof are clearly signposted. During the period in which the park is open a number of regular trains make special stops at Lisse, although it is advisable to ask about these at the booking office.

The gardens are formally laid out and separated by lawns, paths and small lakes where wild ducks land and take off. Flowering trees shade many of the plants and the whole glorious vista of multi-coloured blossoms has a backdrop of natural woodland. There are two gigantic greenhouses containing some 50,000 tulips, where the colours are so vivid that you half close your eyes to take in their beauty. You can visit a pavilion and watch flower arrangement demonstrations and see photographic exhibitions. Contemporary sculptures are among the flower beds and have become a regular feature.

Tulips

It is intriguing to read so many English names on the flowers and it would be interesting to know exactly why each one was chosen. One is Shakespeare (it is red and white striped), another Florence Nightingale, and yet another Queen Victoria. Although Keukenhof is very crowded during the season, there is accommodation for 8000 cars, not to mention fleets of coaches from all over Europe.

Fighting flower pests, developing new and exotic colours and crossing plants keep the horticulturalists occupied. The Dutch have founded the State Bulb Research Centre and Horticultural School near Lisse and here they grow experimental blooms and learn to control various plant diseases. Lifting of the bulbs is done during June and July and this is a very busy time. Eel worms, which attack daffodil and narcissus bulbs, can be eradicated with hot water which does not damage the bulb in any way. The threat of virus, which can affect tulips and was prevalent during Holland's Golden Age, can also be controlled. Tulips painted by many of the great masters can be seen by an expert to have been suffering from the virus attack. Bulbs must be perfect for export and the laboratories see that they are.

It is extraordinary that the glamorous tulip, introduced to Holland from Turkey about 1550 as a collector's item, should now be big business bringing thousands of guilders from abroad each year. The Turks cultivated them in flower beds and used the flowers as patterns on rugs, ceramic tiles, fountains and even tombstones. Their name for the tulip was *lale*, but another Turkish word, *dulband*, (meaning turban) is the origin of our English name, presumably because of the flower's shape.

Dumas' novel *The Black Tulip* caused much controversy. Although this colour did not exist it suddenly became desirable above all others. Even to this day it has not been bred but when it is it will have an immediate impact. The nearest to black is probably the deep plum, curly-edged Black Parrot.

Having asked many people how to keep tulips for as long as possible, I find the answer seems to be to cut the flowers above the white base of the stems. Then roll the individual blooms completely in wet newspaper for an hour or two, to keep the stems straight, before arranging them. If they show signs of wilting they may be lifted out of the vase, have their stems recut and be plunged to the neck in water in a cool, dark place until they have revived.

Leiden

Leiden, with its observatory, botanical gardens and many museums, is a mere 25 miles (40 km) from Amsterdam. It is also the birthplace of such great painters as Rembrandt, Lucas van Leyden, Jan Steen, Gerard Douw and Van Meiris. It edges the southern end of the bulb growing region that stretches from Haarlem. The soil is sandy and, unusual in Holland, well drained. Leiden itself has a special meaning for Americans because of its link with the Pilgrim Fathers. They landed in Amsterdam but discovered that the two English churches already founded there could not agree amongst themselves, so decided to seek asylum elsewhere. They chose Leiden, and requested permission to go there. The Leiden council agreed to welcome them if they would abide by the local laws. The pilgrims mingled with the community, found it to their liking and entered various trades.

Although the pilgrims enjoyed the life in Leiden and recorded it as 'a sweet situation', they knew there was little chance of returning to England or to stay under existing conditions and so they decided to go to the New World. In July 1620 they went by barge to Delfshaven. The next day they sailed to Southampton where they boarded the *Mayflower*.

The Delfshaven chuch where the pilgrims prayed before setting off on their great adventure is a well-known spot for photographers. There is a monument to John Robinson in Leiden and at his church, St Peter's, a memorial service to the pilgrims is held every Thanksgiving Day. John Robinson was in too poor health to accompany the pilgrims on the *Mayflower* and five years later he died. He is buried in the church. The Leiden Municipal Archives museum to the Pilgrim Fathers is open from Monday to Friday from 9 a.m. until noon and 2 to 4 p.m. all the year round.

19 *Leiden Town Hall*

Leiden University

The story of the origin of Leiden's university, the oldest in Holland, is
unique. In 1574 a Spanish detachment laid siege to the town. The citizens
held on doggedly and the Spanish determined to starve them out. After
some months the Dutch were desperate, many perished from hunger, but

20 Hofjes *in Leiden*

they gave no sign of yielding. Their plight was well-known to William of Orange who received heart-rending messages by carrier pigeon at his headquarters in Delft. He was having his own difficulties with the Spanish, but he and his ragged army made valiant attempts to reach the beleaguered town. Finally the only answer left was the one the Dutch always leave as a last resort – flooding the land.

It was a gamble which paid off. Sluice gates were opened and the surging waters flowed quickly and inundated whole areas of south Holland. Over what had only a few days before been green meadows, William and his men sailed to the rescue in their gunboats. The day before relief came, a boy in Leiden, Ewort Joppensz, crawled out through a hole in the town wall and found that the Spanish encampment was deserted. They had discovered that William's forces were on the way. More important to the youngster was a pot the enemy had left behind. It was full to the brim with beef, onions and carrots. He took this back through the wall and today you can see the stewpot in the Cakenhall Museum.

The day after the boy's escapade, on 3 October, William's relief force arrived and with them stores of bread and herrings. On 3 October each year from that time there is a local holiday in Leiden. Nobody can forget why this day is celebrated and a local committee gives out free gifts of herrings and loaves of white bread.

As a mark of his esteem William the Silent offered Leiden the choice of no taxes or a university. After such an auspicious founding Leiden University became famous. Set up in 1575 it was the first of its kind in Holland. Among its better-known teachers have been Arminius, Grotius and Descartes, the French philosopher. The university was very independent and has kept many of its unique rights. It is a striking building with long pointed windows, tiled floors and oak-beamed ceilings. It was originally located in the convent of St Barbara, which was destroyed in 1616. Portraits of famous professors since its earliest days caused Niebuhr to call it the most memorable place in the history of science. The library is rich with Oriental and Greek manuscripts and its fine botanical gardens were founded in 1567. Law and medicine are its most celebrated faculties. It is said that the biographer of Dr Johnson, James Boswell, refused to study law there when his father suggested it, fearing his nose would be kept too close to the grindstone; he chose Utrecht instead.

All students know of the Sweating Room. Over the entrance is written 'Abandon hope all ye that enter here'. It is the place where students go after they have sat their examinations. Generations of them have waited here for their results and scrawled their signatures or drawn on the walls. This is permitted today and among the signatures you will find that of Queen Beatrix. Queen Juliana was also a student here. Renowned names include those of Churchill and Smuts, both of whom received honorary doctorates from Leiden. The university invites visiting professors to give a lecture, and this is carried out under very formal conditions. The lecturer is accompanied to the platform by the whole faculty in full regalia, including a hat of the type worn by Martin Luther, to speak for exactly one hour. If he falls short of this he is considered not to know his subject. If he overruns the hour he may be accused of 'waffling'.

Texel Island

Texel Island is a two hour drive from Amsterdam including a 15 minute ferry crossing. There is seldom long to wait to catch the next hourly drive-on-drive-off boat and no need to book a place. It is the southernmost of the offshore islands along Holland's north-west coast in the Waddenzee, and the most heavily populated with seven villages.

Its chief attraction is for ornithologists, but it is becoming increasingly popular as a camping area. The keen bird watcher might count up to 120 different species including marsh harriers, red shanks, black tailed godwits and colonies of bitterns and terns. There are wild fowl and waders, and the shallow lakes and moorland provide breeding grounds which are carefully protected. The local VVV can supply a brochure on the bird life.

4
THE HAGUE
AND
DELFT

The Hague

The Hague must be one of the most unusual cities in Europe. Edged by formal forests it is sometimes referred to as the biggest or most beautiful village in Europe. In sharp contrast to the embassies and government buildings are the imposing office blocks of Royal Dutch Shell, the N.V. Rubberfabriek Vredestein – the largest rubber industry in the Benelux group – and other industrial firms. As well as parliament buildings, palaces, mansions, tree-lined avenues and well laid out parks there are quiet canals where patient fishermen sit along the banks. Nearby are the bathing resorts of Scheveningen and Kijkduin.

The Hague has never been officially designated as a city and, when a new king or queen is inaugurated, the ceremony is in Amsterdam, the capital of the Netherlands. The Hague came into being by 'sporting' means. Count William II was fond of a hunting lodge inherited from his family in a small settlement known as the *Haagse* (hedge). The surrounding forest was full of game and, being an avid hunter, he decided it was a most suitable place for a castle. After this was built in 1248 it became a focal point for various functions. The court followed William's example and gradually a series of mansions, set in parkland, was erected. From this beginning The Hague emerged and today it has 600,000 inhabitants.

Count William's son, Floris V, had more grandiose ideas than his father and built the vast Binnenhof, surrounded by a great moat, which houses the Dutch parliament today in its magnificent complex of buildings. The splendid 118 ft (35 m) long Hall of the Knights, spanned with slender Gothic arches, is now the archives of the Home Office. Here Queen Beatrix opens the new session of Parliament annually on the third Tuesday in September. The Queen enters her state coach from the Palace of Golden Balconies on her way to the ceremonial opening. The coach is drawn by eight matched horses and escorted by coachmen and footmen in blue and gold livery with tricorn hats.

The small Palace of Golden Balconies was built for the Queen's great-grandmother and nestles next to two of the narrowest houses in The

21 *The former Naval Headquarters at The Hague*

Hague which are only two windows wide. A broad carriageway leads away from it to the Binnenhof, and converging on it also is an avenue bordered by lime trees, the longest in Europe. The Royal Theatre is on the left, a grey and white building which sweeps around a corner in a semicircle.

The old moat which used to surround the Binnenhof has gone, but spread before it is the charming lake of Hofvijver with a small island in the centre and a fountain to one side.

22 *The Binnenhof*

Ridderzaal or Knight's Hall

This building, part of the Binnenhof, which is a maze of palaces, courtyards and gateways, was built in 1280. It is considered one of the finest Gothic buildings in northern Europe. It has witnessed many great occasions, some of them almost unbelievable. One took place at Christmas in 1295 when Count Floris V invited 40 of his richest noblemen to dine and, after a magnificent meal, knighted them and gave each a coat-of-arms. In 1432 and 1456 the historic hall was the rendezvous for feasts accompanying the meetings of the council of the Knights of the Golden Fleece. During these celebrations the escutcheons of the knights were installed in St Jacob's church. These colourful shields are still there. This order of gallantry is probably based on the Greek myth of Jason and the Argonauts, who went on a quest for the Golden Fleece. In their turn the Dutch knights vowed to defend their faith, protect the Holy Church and uphold virtue and morality. The sovereign in return undertook to consult the knights before embarking on a war. All disputes between them were to be settled by the Order.

Charles the Bold was the first to use the Ridderzaal for more than mere feasting. He administered justice there to his subjects who listened while seated on long oak benches. In June 1907 worldwide coverage was given to the Ridderzaal when the second peace conference, sponsored by Tsar Nicholas II, attracted many foreign press men. Winston Churchill inaugurated the West European Alliance there 41 years later. In November 1969 television cameras and telex machines were introduced giving out reports to dozens of newspapers on the European Economic Community summit deliberations.

Among this mass of government buildings is an aged prison, Gevangenpoot, where instruments of torture are still on display. The de Witt brothers, Johan and Cornelius, were dragged from this prison in 1672 and lynched because of their political views. Their tombs and that of the philosopher Spinoza are in the early seventeenth-century New Church not far away. A large square called the Plein is on the opposite side of the Binnenhof, edged by more government buildings including the ornate Ministry of Justice, the large clubhouse of the de Witt Society and the Mauritshuis. In the centre stands a statue of William the Silent with his right foot resting lightly on his pet dog which refused to leave him even in death.

The Mauritshuis

The Mauritshuis was built by Count John Maurice of Nassau in 1633. It is also called the Sugar Palace because Count John was governor of Brazil when he made his fortune from the sugar trade. Some 150 years ago it became a Royal Picture Gallery when William I donated 80 paintings. Some of these were taken by Napoleon, but were eventually retrieved from the Louvre.

The Mauritshuis is one of the most famous picture galleries in Holland and has some 300 paintings, including the largest collection of Rembrandts in the world – boasting one more than the Rijksmuseum in Amsterdam! The building is beautifully proportioned with a Renaissance façade and square, high rooms. Some of the smaller rooms contain only one or two pictures so that nothing else detracts from them.

Probably the most famous Rembrandt is *The Anatomy Lesson* depicting eight bearded medical men clustered round a corpse, their rosy cheeks contrasting vividly with the white skin of the body. Rembrandt painted this work at the early age of 26. The gripping impact of this somewhat distasteful subject is made by the serene face of the dead man, the avid interest of the onlookers and the suggestion of the deft and precise movements of the surgeon as he explains what he is doing. For some reason he wears a hat and has an embroidered white collar, while his students have white ruffles about their necks. This portrait has always been a subject for conjecture, and Glen Tebley, of the Dutch Ballet Company, wrote a ballet called *The Anatomy Lesson* which begins with a tableau of Rembrandt's picture. The corpse revives and the ballet is the story of his life. The performance ends with the same tableau.

As in many museums there are self-portraits of Rembrandt. The four in the Mauritshuis span about 40 years and, although the last one the artist did was of an aged and disillusioned man, the most attractive is of him in fancy dress, wearing a becoming dark velvet hat with plumes. In this he is young and happy and has taken on the character of his costume, even to wearing long gold earrings with a jaunty air.

Saul and David is another outstanding Rembrandt. The boy David is playing his harp, dreamily looking into space. On the other side of a brown velvet curtain, the edge of which has been gathered into Saul's hand to wipe his tears, the king sits overcome by the music. His robes are exotic, comprising a long red velvet cloak and a magnificent multi-coloured silken turban surmounted by a small crown.

Although the parquet floors are bare and shiny, there is an intimate atmosphere in this small museum where every picture is a gem. The lighting is diffused through frosted glass in the ceilings.

Of the three works by Vermeer, *View of Delft* is the most delightful. Rain clouds have just dispersed and left the little township sparkling in pale sunlight as if every building has just been freshly painted. His *Head of a Girl* (sometimes known as *The Girl with a pearl in her ear*) is near the exit and was painted when the artist could afford no more paint. He mixed what he had with water and the result is that with time the surface has cracked. Yet this does not detract from the young girl's winning glance as she dares the onlooker not to notice the large opalescent pearl dangling from her ear. It practically rests on her shoulder.

There is a small room with paintings by Troost (1697–1750). Although his subjects are interiors with people either dancing, laughing or eating together, they have an air of sadness due to his sombre grey overtones. Paulus Potter's *Young Bull* is a very realistic painting; a farmer is standing in the shade of a tree where a couple of sheep and a white-faced cow are resting, while the bull stands alongside. A story goes that an Arab sheik booked a suite at the Hotel Krasnapolsky many years ago, and demanded that it should contain a cow so that he could have fresh milk every day. Although this was impossible the manager thought some gesture should be made and had a copy of the *Young Bull* hung in the suite.

As with many picture galleries in Holland there are two or three paintings of the church in Delft which was built in the fourteenth century. In it are all the tombs of the Royal House of Orange, including a grandiose one made for William the Silent. This monument is flanked by columns and is a favourite subject for painters. Whether because William's pet dog lies at his feet or not, dogs are always shown frisking in the interior of the church. Two of these paintings at the Mauritshuis are by Houckgeest, and in one you can see the tomb of William through the pillars while bright sunlight pours in through the vaulted windows.

The Peace Palace
As in Cairo the Sphinx proves as fascinating as the Pyramids, so in The Hague the Peace Palace draws visitors as much as the stately buildings of the Binnenhof. It is a tangible sign of man's desire to banish war and many countries have helped to establish it.

The Hague became a centre for treaties between nations almost as soon as it came into being. In 1609 a truce was signed between the Netherlands and Spain; Denmark agreed to an alliance in 1666; and 1668 produced a Triple Alliance between the Netherlands, England and Sweden. A second Triple Alliance was signed in 1710 and yet another with France, England and the Netherlands in 1717. Peace was agreed there in the same year between Spain, Austria and Savoy. The International Peace Conference met at The Hague in 1889 and again in 1907. It was in 1901 that the idea of a Palace of Peace, to be the permanent seat of the International Court of Arbitration, became a reality. Andrew Carnegie, a Scottish weaver who went to America to seek his fortune and became a millionaire, contributed £300,000 towards the cost of the building.

Twenty international architects sent in designs for the project and two of them, a Frenchman, Louis Cordonnier, and a Dutchman, Van der Steur, were chosen to do the work. Each country which belonged to The Hague Convention made a presentation. The foundation stone, granite from Bavaria, was laid by a representative of Nicholas II of Russia. The Tsar personally gave a gigantic $3\frac{1}{2}$ ton vase of green jasper, which stands in the centre of an ante-room off the small Court of Justice. Belgium sent bronze doors; gilt chandeliers came from Austria; tapestries from France and Japan; stained-glass windows from Britain; a carved figure of Christ from Argentina; tables from Brazil; four magnificent vases from China, and in all 64 countries sent gifts. Italy contributed the Carrara marble which paves the entrance hall and has an inscription reading 'Son of Justice Light our Path'. The surrounding gardens were sketched and planned by Mawson, a British landscape gardener, and two large wrought-iron gates leading to them were donated by Germany.

Should you wish to check the time when visiting the Peace Palace there is an unusual clock in its tower. It was the gift of Switzerland and is

controlled electronically from Basle. It is precise to a thousandth of a
second and guaranteed never to gain or lose.

The Peace Palace is large containing 83 rooms, 11 halls and a library
boasting 500,000 books. Thousands of visitors go round on guided tours
annually. The furnishings are colourful, with blue predominating, but in
the conference room off the large Hall of Justice – where 50 judges can sit
on occasion – the colours are muted and the walls are covered with
brown and beige cut velvet. The place seemed to lack nothing until I
asked before leaving where the kitchens were. 'We have no kitchens' said
the guide. 'If anyone gets hungry there is quite a good restaurant nearby!'

Places of interest
The Hague, with its tree-lined avenues, grassy squares and gardens, is
one of the greenest towns in the Netherlands. Its woods have been
described as its finest ornament and may well be the remains of those
which once stretched along the coastline. Only ten minutes from the
heart of the city you can be in them at Wassenaar. Here oak, alder and
beech trees are sometimes aproned by small lakes, and there are beautiful
mansions in various styles. In 250 acres (100 ha) of wood and parkland is
the Duinrell Leisure and Camping Park facing the sea.

Back in The Hague there are several places where you can enjoy
Indonesian dishes. At the Des Indes hotel the grill room has achieved
mention in several food guides and rightly so. As in Vienna there are
famous pastry shops where you can sip coffee, tea or hot chocolate, and
conversation mainly centres on which of the various delicacies placed
temptingly in front of you should be chosen first.

Nordeinde Street has shops selling luxury articles of all kinds and there
are several antique dealers. The street widens into a small square before
continuing. Set back on the right-hand side is the charming small Palace
Nordeinde. Before it is a bronze statue of King William I which has
weathered to a lichen green. He wears a ruff about his neck and his hat is
set at a jaunty angle. Behind the King's statue is a small open space with a
spreading orange tree, beneath which a market is run by men and boys on
Saturday afternoons.

Leaving the square behind you, continue along the shopping street
which eventually opens into a larger space across which you can see one
of The Hague's three Town Halls. It is picturesque with an open bell
tower. The corner café, the Golden Hat Inn, is dated 1660 and has a
brown wooden musician's gallery surrounding the main floor.

A most unusual type of picture gallery is not far away in Zeestraat –
Sea Street – called Panorama Mesdag. You enter through rooms hung
with paintings by Hendrick Mesdag, his wife and others of his school,
such as Breitner. Their speciality was seascapes with storms and grey

skies. These sombre pictures and a long dark corridor do not prepare you for the delightful panorama which suddenly confronts you. You climb a short staircase and find yourself on a round fenced platform surrounded by a vast circular canvas. It is a panorama of Scheveningen and The Hague as they were in 1881, 45 ft (14 m) high and 400 ft (122 m) wide. Between you and the picture is a stretch of real sand dotted with anchors, nets, wooden clogs and other things you might spot on the sea-shore.

Hendrik William Mesdag painted this extraordinary canvas in four months. His wife added the houses and a friend did a detachment of cavalry exercising their horses at the water's edge 'to give the picture more movement'. The whole scene is sunlit; birds fly overhead and skim the waves, flat-bottomed fishing boats have been dragged up on the sand and fishermen tend their nets. A lighthouse is far out on a spit of land and eastward is The Hague with rows of stately houses.

Mesdag was born in 1831 in Groningen and studied art in Brussels. He settled in The Hague in 1869. Having independent means he was able to form a small school of artists who also indulged in his favourite subject – immensity and boundless space of sea and sky.

Theatre and music lovers are not forgotten in The Hague and the Congress Centre has three theatres and a concert hall. One theatre has been panelled in teak and the stage has six adjustable platforms. There are six smaller halls on the ground floor of the main building of the Centre and it has underground parking for 800 cars. The Hague Council and the Dutch Government have put 18 million dollars into this project. The outer walls of this ultra modern building are sky-blue and yellow with a large Picasso-style mural on the façade. Incongruous chimneys are camouflaged by a tower containing flats.

Hotel des Indes
One of the most historic buildings is the Hotel des Indes, now a Crest hotel. It is popular with diplomats as it is in the embassy area. It was built in 1851 as the residence of Baron van Brienen van de Groote Linat and was extended in 1881. Extensive refurbishing in recent years has combined the elegance of the past with the modern comforts expected nowadays. It is within a few minutes walk of The Hague Central Station, which has a direct connection with Schiphol airport, and close to motorways to Amsterdam, Utrecht and Rotterdam. The Hague's museums are also within easy reach of it, and the Mauritshuis is only three minutes walk away.

The hotel was the former town house of the van Brienens, who also had a country estate close to the sea called Huize Clingendael. William Joseph van Brienen had the grounds laid out on what he considered 'romantic English style'. In 1895 Margaret Mary van Brienen visited

Japan and, on her return, added a Japanese tea garden. While abroad she had acquired not only materials for the bridges, but also stone lanterns, a tea house and a porter's lodge. Azaleas and maples were planted; little streams and pools were laid out; a Buddha mused beside a water pot. When the garden was finished the Baroness received her guests standing on a mat of moss, which in Japan symbolized welcome.

During the Second World War, after the death of the Baroness, the property was requisitioned by a Nazi Gauleiter and the garden fell into neglect. In 1975 the Dutch Ministry of Foreign Affairs aided by the Ministry of Culture, the provincial authorities and the municipality of Wassenaar, agreed to spend 12 million guilders on the estate and, during six weeks in May and June when the Japanese garden is at its best, it is open to the public.

Madurodam

No one visiting The Hague should miss Madurodam, Holland's miniature city. It covers 4 acres (1.6 ha) to one side of the canal connecting The Hague with Scheveningen. Everything is on a scale of one twenty-fifth ordinary size. Mr and Mrs Maduro gave it in memory of their son George, a young lieutenant, who died in Dachau concentration camp having been taken prisoner after the heroic resistance to the German invasion in 1940. The profits go to charity.

Madurodam is like a real city, with its own harbour complete with ferries, ships and lighthouse. There is an airport with a runway, terminal buildings and aircraft in the colours of various airlines. Windmills turn and buses move along highways beneath bridges over which trains pass. Many of the main buildings are replicas of real ones seen in Dutch towns so that parts seem familiar to onlookers. The best time to visit is at dusk when the lights come on. Choirs can be heard singing through the lighted stained-glass windows of the cathedral and the lights of the houses are reflected in the canals where barges pass one another. In all 50,000 lights bring the town to life, warning beacons flash on top of the radio tower and the streets are illuminated. As you stroll along the pathways through the town you feel like a giant in comparison. Madurodam even has a live mayor, the Queen's eldest son. It is always advisable to check opening times for museums and places like Madurodam with the local VVV or your hotel porter as they sometimes change.

Scheveningen

From Madurodam, if you continue along by the bank of the same canal that you followed from The Hague, you come to Scheveningen. An old

23 *Madurodam. Note the model 'tree houses' in the foreground*

book written at the turn of the century states that 'Scheveningen is a fashionable seaside resort on the North Sea two miles north west of The Hague with which it is connected by a beautiful walk'. It is still situated in sand dunes at the extremity of The Hague woods but has been absorbed into the city so that, in a sense, The Hague and Scheveningen form a double city each keeping its own characteristics, which differ greatly.

Scheveningen, a fishing port as well as being Holland's largest bathing resort, has an outer and two inner harbours. The fish auction hall covers 10,800 sq yd (9000 sq m). National costumes are worn mostly by the older women. On Sunday mornings you see them going to church in long billowing black skirts and jackets and spotless white caps. These are held in place by large hatpins, one either side of the forehead, topped with solid gold buttons of intricate design. These are handed down from generation to generation and contrast with the sober costumes. They are practically impossible to buy and are highly treasured; once again an attractive oriental detail plays so much a part of Dutch dressing.

It was off Scheveningen in 1673 that Admiral de Ruyter defeated the combined English and French fleets. After the Napoleonic Wars in 1813, William I came ashore at Scheveningen, and this event is commemorated

24   *The seaside resort of Scheveningen*

by an obelisk. It looks strangely out of place amongst the dunes.

The 2 mile (3 km) long Strandweg is fringed with hotels, cafés and restaurants. The new pier, which was finished in 1961, juts 1200 ft (365 m) out to sea and has an underwater panorama, a children's playground, amusement centres and a 150 ft (46 m) high observation tower. There is a regular passenger ferry service to the east coast of Britain.

The fishing harbour has the largest herring fleet in Holland, and, by tradition, the first barrel of fresh herring landed at the beginning of the season is presented to the Queen and the Lord Mayor.

Some time after 1818, when Jacob Pronck built the first bathing establishment at Scheveningen, important foreigners came to bathe and take the cure. Some years later the Kurhaus Hotel came into being, situated on a bluff overlooking the sea.

Kurhaus Hotel
The Kurhaus Hotel celebrated its centenary in 1985. It was built during the days of the Grand Tour when Scheveningen was very different. It was a time of horse-drawn carriages and slow-moving trains. People wore hats and carried umbrellas to protect them from the sun. Holiday

makers went into the sea in bath chairs, little girls wore long dresses, and small boys sailor suits and white round caps with ribbon streamers.

Royalty and heads of state used the Kurhaus Hotel as a rendezvous; the bedrooms were spacious and beautifully furnished, the reception rooms elegant. Life went by at a leisurely pace and even in the late 6os dinner was not served in the main restaurant until 10 p.m.

After the depressing war days of the 1940s the hotel had a brief revival, but now generations of tourists wanted a different way of life on holiday and it closed down in 1973. However Scheveningen without its Kurhaus was inconceivable and it was decided to remodel much of the building, retaining its comfort and charm. It was reopened in 1979 and guests can now enjoy fashion shows, dance galas and concerts. La Coquille, the *haute cuisine* restaurant, overlooks the sea, and businessmen and government officials can use the new conference centre. In the meantime the Kurhaus' casino, the largest in the Netherlands, has become the busiest on the North Sea coast.

Restaurants

There are numerous eating places ranging from gourmet restaurants to fast food bars. The Buffeterie with a superb view over the promenade, beach and sea, can accommodate 450 people. In this unusual self-service establishment, the only one of its kind in Holland, you can take your choice of sandwiches, Mexican tacos, Indonesian, Chinese or Surinamese specialities, pizzas, snacks and fish platters. Desserts are numerous and you can choose between puddings, exotic sherbets or ice cream. Dutch dishes, such as the famous pancakes and pea soup, are not forgotten.

There is a local restaurant classification system in the form of Scheveningen Starfish awards. Five starfish are given for true excellence and so on down the scale. You can be sure that the fresh fish in a five star restaurant will be delicious.

Of the Scheveningen monuments the most appealing perhaps is the statue of a fisherman's wife looking out to sea waiting for the return of the fishing fleet. It was unveiled by Queen Beatrix in November 1982 and commemorates the many fishermen who over the years have lost their lives at sea.

The Fisherschurch dating from 1450 has two great whale jawbones just inside the entrance and is known for its excellent acoustics.

Many tours are available and an unusual one is a visit to watch the artisan candlemakers at work. After being guided round you can make your own candle by the centuries-old immersion method. Of course you can buy many kinds of moulded or immersion candles at the shop before leaving.

Shopping is an event in itself seven days a week and often also in the evenings. The roofed-in Palace Promenade is especially convenient if it is raining because there are tea rooms and restaurants as well.

Among the sporting pursuits are sailing and water skiing, and sail catamarans are available with instructors.

Delft

Known for its exquisite blue china since the seventeenth and eigthteenth centuries, Delft is midway between The Hague and Rotterdam. A very quiet place after the bustle of Scheveningen, it is considered the loveliest little city in Holland and a mecca for artists. It is almost Venetian with its many canals, except that they are mostly tree-lined. Many of the narrow pavements are made of small stonework in unusual turquoise, dull yellow and grey. These muted colours, enhanced by a canal down the middle of almost every street, shed a luminosity like an artist's palette. Little white wrought-iron bridges span the canals and during summer the banks are colour-streaked with flowers. The tiniest bridge of all, only a few feet long, is known as the Butter Bridge.

Delft is a place for walking, and you cannot do better than follow a route suggested by the Dutch Tourist Office (who have an office in the square). It takes in many of the interesting places to see and is in the most picturesque part of the city. If you begin in the market square you can see the Town Hall with its gay red shutters and gilded ornamentation opposite the New Church. The sides of the square fringing these two buildings are bordered with cafés and shops. Then walk down the left side of the Town Hall and along the canals until you come upon the Paul Tatar Museum.

Situated in the Koornmarkt it is an old patrician mansion which belonged to a rich painter of that name and is left furnished as it was during the artist's lifetime. He was a dedicated follower of Vermeer. Paul Tatar married twice, but had no children, and when he died he left his house to the nation. It is full of period Dutch furniture and on every flat surface there are vases and ceramics, mostly Delft ware. His study is lined with Italian tooled leather, each wall having a different intricate design. Delft tiles are used as skirting board in the upper floor.

If you return to the back of the Town Hall and keep to the right you will immediately see the Old Church, behind which is the Prinsenhof; to the right of this famous museum, once a fifteenth-century monastery, there is the Huis Lambert van Meerten Museum.

The New Church, with its splendid tower, actually dates from 1384 and took a century to complete; for generations it has been the burial place of the Royal family. It is renowned for its allegorical monument to

William the Silent which is enclosed by 22 slender white pillars and has always been a favourite subject for artists. At the King's feet rests his pet dog, which refused to eat when his master died. The monument was designed by Hendrik de Keyser and his son Pieter about 1627 and, beneath this great edifice, in the crypt lie the other members of the House of Orange.

25   *The New Church at Delft*

The Old Church contains the tombs of Admirals Piet Hein and Maarten Tromp, both famous in the seventeenth century, and the naturalist Leeuwenhoek, born in 1632 in Delft.

The Prinsenhof

The Prinsenhof during the fifteenth century was the wealthiest convent in Holland, when it was known as St Agatha's Nunnery. In 1575 it was converted into a residence for the Princes of Orange and, within its quiet walls, William the Silent was assassinated. It is now a museum, part of which is dedicated to the liberation of Holland. It contains many paintings of land and sea battles and in another section there is a montage of the Royal Family consisting of documents, paintings and mementos.

The museum walls are whitewashed and austere and there is a simple chapel containing a triptych, the centre panel of which is carved wood while the outer ones are painted. The scene in the centre shows the birth of Christ with the Holy Child and crib in the foreground. The two paintings are of Christ with his Mother, and Mary being visited by Gabriel. Choir stalls are behind three arches at the far end of the chapel.

All the rooms in the Prinsenhof are engaging. There are several paintings of the New Church and it is interesting to compare them. There is a hall of Flemish tapestries and, just outside this, there is the circular staircase where King William was killed. Glass covers two bullet holes in the old wall, one much deeper than the other.

The Huis Lambert van Pauw

The Huis Lambert van Pauw has Holland's most perfect collection of old Dutch tiles and is furnished in nineteenth-century style. It is spacious, charming and very colourful as the tiles are in every hue. They feature flowers, birds, geometrical designs and other patterns, and come not only from Holland but also from the rest of Europe and the Far East.

Light streams through many windows all with inside shutters embellished with ornate brass fittings and locks. The fireplaces are lined with multi-coloured tiles and they hang along the walls and up a square staircase reaching to a skylight in the roof. The first floor has carved wooden ceilings. The carved wooden banisters have candlesticks at each turning. The square skylight has 12 stained-glass windows depicting the signs of the Zodiac. Tiles are used as paintings, including some from Spain and Persia. One room is three-sided – like a South African stoop – with a view on to a formal garden.

Delft ware

You can visit factories and watch the blue and white china being made. The old pieces are signed with a stylized *f* sandwiched between a wide vase with a straight line along its opening and the word 'Delft'. In addition they sometimes have the initials of the individual artist. The making of faïence became one of the eight crafts of Delft which formed the Guild of St Luke in 1611. Although it is known that Herman Pietersz of Haarlem introduced it to Delft, it is not certain where he learned the craft. By 1650 it had become so refined and celebrated that Delft was producing the best ceramics in Northern Europe.

There is no doubt that the Chinese – perhaps the greatest potters ever known with their world-famous translucent porcelain – inspired faïence makers everywhere. In Delft during the seventeenth century Dutch potters successfully captured the colour values of Chinese white and blue porcelain. As their fame spread other European countries tried to imitate them. It was not until the French occupation at the end of the eighteenth century that the art began to wane.

In recent years the Royal Factory at Delft has been resuscitated and today there are many artists producing beautiful work. It is interesting to the onlooker that before glazing and firing the Delft blue is, in fact, a drab grey. Red and plain white work is now also popular.

Probably because Delft is renowned for its china an annual antique fair is held there. Thousands of visitors pass through the Prinsenhof Museum to see the displays of Dutch and international dealers. The fair is usually held during the last few days of June and the beginning of July.

Vermeer

Johannes Vermeer (born in 1632) is Delft's most renowned painter and was greatly influenced by Pieter de Hooch, of the same town but three years older. Both artists enjoyed portraying house interiors with sunlight filtering through windows and housewives going about their domestic chores. One of the most charming pictures by de Hooch, *The Pantry*, is in the Rijksmuseum. An enchanting little flaxen-haired girl, in a long dress with white collar and cuffs and bonnet to match, is holding up her hands to take a jug from her mother, who has just left the pantry. The mother seems amused at the gravity of the girl. The sun shines through windows onto chequered flooring and picks out the tiled skirting board. A door is open to the right showing another room where the portrait of a man is accented by sunlight from a window. It is as though the hall door was ajar and, passing by, your eyes are drawn to the pleasing scene.

The house interiors of Vermeer are the perfect housewife's dream: well-made furniture shines with polish, mirrors and tiles gleam and floors are spotless. The women have a milkmaid freshness and are tastefully dressed. No one could catch them unaware, nor are they in a hurry. Even in his *A Street in Delft* no passer-by could startle the woman contentedly sitting and embroidering lace in her sunlit doorway; there is no sense of urgency emanating from the maid soaking clothes in a water butt. Vermeer brings the same eye for detail and freshness to his outdoor work, which often looks as if there has just been a shower of rain to brighten everything up.

5

DRINK AND FOOD

Drink

The Dutch are said to be hearty eaters, and this is true. They insist on generous helpings, a pancake can measure 1 ft (30 cm) across and their drink must have plenty of 'body'. *Advocaat*, of far more syrupy consistency than most liqueurs, is served with a little spoon. It is described sometimes as a ladies' drink, perhaps because years ago every Dutch housewife had her own family recipe.

Gin, unknown in England until the middle of the seventeenth century, was first distilled in Holland and for a long time was known internationally as 'Hollands'. The name *genever* (which is where the word gin derives from) means juniper, as the juniper berry is the main flavouring agent. If you order *genever* you will be given a small glass of straight gin. You can have *old genever* or *new genever*, the first stronger than the last. The Dutchman usually likes to sip his gin as an aperitif before a meal and the story goes that the habit grew because a glass or two will keep out the damp of the canals in winter!

'Pleasure shared is pleasure doubled' say the Dutch and they enjoy drinking and eating with their family and intimate friends in their own homes rather than at restaurants. *Genever* can be served at any time. Although Dutch women join their husbands for a pre-dinner drink in the evenings they are supposed to prefer *citroengenever* (lemon gin) or *bessengenever* (blackcurrant gin) to plain *genever*. If sugar is added to *citroengenever* it is served with a small spoon like *advocaat*. Both *bessengenever* and *citroengenever* are very good in long drinks with soda, ice and a little lemon peel added.

The oldest and best-known name in Dutch gin is Bols and when, in 1575, Lucas Bols asked permission to build a distillery in Amsterdam, his request was refused by the burgomaster because of the fire risk which would be created by open burners. Bols was not deterred and started a small factory in the city outskirts which eventually became the foundation of today's enormous premises.

Wynand Fockink

Several years ago, when visiting Amsterdam, my father took me to the famous 'tasting' bar Wynand Fockink. It is the smallest of bars and the first I had ever visited. I found it very romantic. It was dimly lit and the walls were lined with green shelves which held dozens of hand-painted and strangely shaped bottles, some of them hundreds of years old. A pot-bellied stove blazed away in one corner and the bar itself was of scrubbed wood. A tiny trough with gurgling water stood in the middle like a small fountain for washing up. Glistening cone-shaped glasses stood on either side. These were filled to the brim with any type of gin liqueur that a customer ordered but were not to be lifted up by hand. Visitors had to observe the rule of the house by bending over the bar and taking the first sip without raising the glass. If this was not done it could cost the customer drinks all round. I was given three amusing postcards by the proprietor. The first showed two men sipping Wynand Fockink's most popular drink, 'half and half', bending over the bar. In the second card they were having their second glass with their legs off the ground and in the last one, taking their third drink, their legs were floating in the air.

When I revisited the bar a few months ago it was exactly the same as I remembered it, but no postcards were given away. However, there was a framed picture of the same men drinking their 'half and half', and their background was of the same bottles. To find this bar you take a turning beyond the Grand Hotel Krasnapolsky off the Dam Square and it is in a small alley called Pijlsteeg.

Not far away is another tasting bar, the Tip van Bootz, where the same ceremony of bending over the bar to take your first sip is observed. Its speciality is a vivid red liqueur called Tip van Bootz. The word 'tip' is said to have come into being because stockbrokers used to gather there to exchange financial tips.

Liqueurs

Bols make a liqueur called 'Hansje in den Kelder' (Little Hans in the Cellar). This was inspired by the pregnancy cup which is now an exhibit at the museum in the Bols distillery. A gentleman had it made as an unusual way to announce that his wife was pregnant. There is an inverted bowl in the middle and when liquid was poured into the cup and reached a certain level the bowl opened up revealing a tiny statue of a child.

Modern technology has now taken over, but until a few years ago the way the delicious Dutch liqueur chocolates were made was fascinating. They were filled by hypodermic syringes. The hollow chocolate shapes were injected with the liqueur and then the hole sealed with chocolate. There are two distinct types of liqueur chocolates. One has the casing lined with sugar before the liqueur is added and the other is plain.

Although wines which are mostly imported are expensive, liqueurs, such as Curacao, are reasonable. Wines cost less in Limburg as this province can import direct from the growers in France and Germany.

Beer

Dutch beer is excellent. It is always served very cold and tastes like Czech pilsener. Imported beer can be had anywhere but it costs much more than the local brands. A normal size Dutch beer glass holds about a third of a pint.

Food

Breakfast

Dutch breakfasts are what many people would call a light lunch. In most cases hotel prices include breakfast. Your waiter will bring you a laden tray. A basket invariably contains a mixture of white and brown bread including pumpernickel, ginger bread and honey bread called *ontbijkoek*. Paper-thin slices of beef or veal will be on the same plate as a slice of cheese, which is equally thin. This is done by a special cheese cutter, which looks like a wide cake knife with a scraping blade in the middle. It shaves the cheese into almost transparent wafers. There will be a laden butter dish and at least two different types of jam. Your tea pot will probably be complete with tea cosy and, to enable you to pour it, a small handle cosy is often joined to the larger one so that you will not burn your fingers.

Lunch

Lunch, if you eat like the Dutch, will be somewhat more substantial than breakfast, but is similar in that it has a bread base. Meats, cheese, sausage or fish are served on open slices of bread or more often in a *broodje,* the famous Dutch luncheon roll. Indeed many snack bars are called *broodjes*. A favourite lunch dish is *broodje* covered with sliced ham and topped with a fried egg or two. On cold days, particularly, a cup of soup often starts the lunch, especially the warming pea soup (the recipe for which is given later in this chapter). Another favourite dish is a pancake which can be sweet or savoury. This is a meal in itself, covers a meat plate and is about half an inch thick. It can be stuffed with cheese, vegetables, apples, ginger, jam, crispy bacon and other things. Wine is seldom drunk with a snack, beer or coffee being preferred.

Dinner

Dinner is the main meal of the day, usually served between 6 and 7 p.m. in the home. It is rare for the husband to bring home business acquaintances or important guests. Entertaining of this kind is mostly done in restaurants. Even then dinner can be early as some places close their kitchens before 10 p.m.

It is not only in Holland that plovers' eggs are considered a delicacy, for the Dutch export them to many countries. European crested plovers are protected in the Netherlands and they lay thousands of eggs in northern Friesland during the spring. It is legal to collect the eggs for one month during the season. They are speckled olive green and are found in the nests, pointed-end inwards, in threes or fours. It is said that the hunter who finds the first egg has the pleasure of being able to present it to the Queen.

Fish

Even hundreds of years ago the Dutch were renowned for their smoked eels, but the reclamation of land and water pollution has cut down the supply gradually so that today hundreds of tons of eels are imported. However, ingenuity has solved the problem to some extent. Culverts have been cut in the piers of the Haringvliet dam to allow eels to migrate. They lay their eggs in the Sargasso Sea. When these are hatched the young eels return in their millions and so the life-cycle continues. Smoked eel is as delicious served as an *hors d'oeuvre* as smoked salmon.

Herring stands are as much a part of Dutch cities as barrel organs and are as popular as hot dog stands in America. The herrings are raw and, if you are tempted, you dip them into chopped onions first. If you prefer to have a taste first before tackling the fish in the approved style you can spear a small piece with a tooth pick. The correct way is to pick up the herring by the tail, between thumb and second finger, dip it in the chopped onion and, holding it above your head, lower it into your mouth. Close your mouth, bite off the flesh and draw out the skeleton. It has a piquant flavour which most newcomers claim to enjoy, but I find it too salty.

Cheese

Dutch cheeses are so well known and delicious that they are difficult to resist. In France cheese is usually served before the dessert at dinner parties, in Britain at the end, but in Holland it is preferred at breakfast or lunch. What is not such common knowledge is that the Dutch are inordinately fond of other milk products such as yoghurt and buttermilk. Milk itself often takes the place of coffee or tea. Workmen carry bottles of milk in their lunch baskets. However, cheese is popular at cocktail parties and can be served in various ways and flavours.

Sightseeing boat on an Amsterdam canal

Windmills at Winderdijk

Vrijthof terrace at Maastricht

Recipes

Uitsmijters

Ingredients

6 slices white bread	Butter
6 eggs	Salt, pepper and mustard
12 slices ham or roast beef	Pickles

Method

Butter all the slices of bread, put 2 slices of ham or roast beef on each which should more than cover the bread. Fry the eggs soft and place one on each slice. Serve two on each plate with pepper, salt, mustard and pickles. This is one of Holland's favourite lunch dishes.

Erwtensoep (Dutch pea soup)

Ingredients

2 cups green split peas	6 celery sticks (chopped)
3½ quarts water	½ lb smoked sausage, cubed
2 pig's feet	or coarsely sliced
4 leeks (chopped)	

Method

Soak peas in 3 cups cold water for 12 hours. Drain and add enough water to make 3½ quarts. Add salt and bring to boil. Skim and add pig's feet, leeks and celery. Simmer for 4 to 5 hours or until the pig's feet are quite tender and meat loosens from bones. Add bits of meat to soup. Half an hour before serving add sausage. Strips of toasted bread or dark pumpernickel are eaten with the soup. Serves 8.

Rode Kool (Red cabbage)

Ingredients

1 small red cabbage	3 cloves
½ cup butter	3 cups water
2 cooking apples	1 tablespoon sugar
1 handful rice	salt

Method

Remove outer leaves and cut cabbage in half. Remove core, wash and shred. Boil in water to which butter, rice, peeled and cored apples, salt and cloves have been added. Simmer for 45 minutes. Add sugar, a dash of nutmeg and cinnamon and boil for 5 more minutes.

Speculaaspop (St Nicholas' doll)

Ingredients

3 cups flour
½ cup dark brown sugar
Some milk to soften the dough
¼ teaspoon powdered cloves

⅔ cup butter or margarine
a pinch of baking powder and salt
½ teaspoon nutmeg
½ cup blanched almonds slivered
  (keep some for decoration)

Method

Knead all ingredients except almonds for decorating to a soft ball. Roll out on a floured board to ¼ inch thick. Stamp out shapes or make a gingerbread doll or biscuit. Bake for 25 minutes at 350°F. You can also make them like brownies, cut into squares (bake longer, 30-35 minutes). They are then called *speculaasjes*.

Peppernoten (Peppernuts)

Ingredients

1¼ cups flour
½ cup brown sugar
1 egg yolk
Some anise seeds
A pinch of salt

1¼ cups self raising flour
2 tablespoons water
¼ teaspoon each cinnamon,
  powdered cloves and nutmeg

Method

Knead all ingredients into a soft ball. Butter two baking sheets. Form about 90 marble sized balls. Divide them over the sheets so that they do not touch one another and flatten slightly. Bake for 20 minutes at 350°F or until done, when they are very hard.

Ontbijtkoek (Dutch spice cake)

Ingredients

2 cups self-raising flour
½ cup molasses or treacle
1 cup milk
½ teaspoon grated nutmeg

½ cup dark brown sugar
1 teaspoon each ground cloves,
  cinnamon and ginger
Pinch of salt

Method

Combine all the ingredients into a smooth paste. Butter an 8 in by 3 in cake tin, fill with dough and bake for 1 hour at 300°F. When cooked allow to cool and keep in a tin or breadbin for 24 hours before serving. The Dutch serve this with their 'elevenses' buttered or for breakfast on a slice of bread.

Haringsla (Mixed herring salad)

Ingredients

1 small cooked beetroot	2 cooking apples
Some pickled onions and gherkins	8 cold cooked potatoes
2 hard-boiled eggs	Some lettuce or curly endives
2 tablespoons vinegar	Salt
Mayonnaise	3 fresh herrings

Method

Soak the herrings in milk or water, renewing the liquid at intervals and cleaning and skinning the fish. Bone and cut into small pieces. Keep a few for decorating. Cut peeled beetroot and apples into pieces. Chop the onions, gherkins, potatoes and one egg. Wash the lettuce or endives and shred finely. Put all ingredients into a big bowl. Mix well with salad oil and vinegar and salt. Place the salad on a flat dish and smooth the top with a wet spoon. Coat the salad with mayonnaise and decorate with quarters of egg, pieces of herring and surround with small pieces of inside lettuce leaves. Serve with toast and butter.

Dutch veal steak with cherries and raisins

Ingredients

4½ oz veal steak	2 oz butter
Teaspoon paprika	Cream
Soaked raisins	Stoned cherries

Method

Fry the veal steak in the butter. Add the paprika. When nearly cooked add a dash of cream and a few raisins and cherries. Stew for 5 minutes before serving.

Restaurants

In 1895 Dikker and Company owned a fish and delicatessen shop in Kalverstraat. It was a successful venture and a larger place was bought in the same street. A restaurant was added, and from that day Dikker and Thijs (the erstwhile 'Company', and a pupil of Escoffier) became a renowned restaurant.

It has now moved to the corner of Leidsestraat and Prinsengracht but still retains its delicatessen downstairs. Its famous restaurant is on the first floor. The menu is extensive and every dish is a masterpiece. Snipe are served flamed in brandy. Haunch of hare or pheasant can be roasted or served with cream sauce. Two other luscious dishes are cushions of venison with goose liver pâté, and saddle of venison St Hubert. If guests particularly enjoy something they can sometimes buy a tin or jar of it to take home from the delicatessen downstairs.

Besides the main restaurant and delicatessen the building (at one time a warehouse of several floors) houses the Café du Centre at street level, a superior *broodjes* without the usual snack bar rush. The hot and cold food here is delicious. A 'Snack Baron' consists of veal ragout, egg and grilled cheese.

Christmas is the time when bakers' shops are full of figures of St Nikolas rolled in chocolate, and pastry letters stuffed with almond paste. M is the most popular initial, perhaps because it is the first letter of Christ's mother's name. Possibly more *hopjes,* the famed hard toffee with a coffee flavour, are sent abroad to friends at Christmas than during the rest of the year. They were first exported to Egypt, India and America as early as 1795. Both these delicacies can be sent anywhere in the world from Dikker and Thijs.

One of the most famous steak restaurants in Amsterdam is in Die Port van Cleve Hotel at 178 Nieuwe Zijds, Voorburgwaal next to the main Post Office and just behind the Dam Square. Prices are in the medium range and the hotel has that elusive atmosphere created by aged buildings. Indeed in the days when most waiters could neither read nor write they could not note down the orders. Instead an echo system was used. Orders were called out to an intermediary standing several yards away near the kitchen. He shouted the order to the cooks. This practice was kept up as a gimmick until recently, but it is no longer considered worthwhile. However, one other special inducement remains. From the beginning when the succulent steaks were first served, they were numbered and, by the 1970s, the total had reached more than 5,000,000. Today if your order ends with three zeroes it is on the house. Tourists collect the number of their steak even if it is not free.

If you are in a hurry, but wish to sample some typical Dutch specialities, there are restaurants with the sign 'Neerlands Dis' (there are nearly 200 of them across Holland) where you will find beef hotpot, thick pea soup and other indigenous dishes at reasonable prices. Another tip: if you are hungry enough to need a three course meal, yet wish to conserve your holiday money, there are some 600 restaurants in the country with the sign 'Tourist Menu' outside which are very good. They often include items in season and are well worth a visit. The VVV can supply a list of them.

A travel writer friend of mine, Christine Fagg, was invited to a Dutch lunch in London. The food was delicious but filling. When the time came to choose a dessert Christine thought she had better not indulge in a slice of one of the delectable cakes, not even a petit four. Her eyes lit on a small box on a side table which had a pretty flower design. She opened it. It was full of small bell-shaped chocolates. She popped one in her mouth and bit into it. It had a bitter sour taste so she swallowed it hastily. 'What are these?' she asked. Her host smiled as he walked towards her. 'I have a little box like that for each of my guests to take home,' he said. 'They are miniature tulip bulbs.'

As her husband happens to be a doctor she rang him immediately. He advised that it was unlikely to prove fatal but she should not make a practice of it!

6
UTRECHT

Utrecht is the smallest province in the Netherlands. Low and fertile, with several of the tributaries of the Rhine crossing it, it lies south of the Zuyder Zee. Its capital is also Utrecht, which was the centre of the Jansenist (or Old Catholic) religious party of Holland, and the seat of their archbishop. For good reason the name Utrecht brings the treaty of that name to mind. After the great European war of the Spanish Succession, the series of treaties signed there in 1713 and 1714 gave England possession of Newfoundland, Nova Scotia and Gibraltar. This led to her gradual expansion and overseas commercial prosperity.

The cathedral, known as the Dom, was partially destroyed during a hurricane in 1674 when the nave was blown down. It seems a strange quirk of fate that the tower should escape damage as it is still the highest in the Netherlands. For some reason the nave was not rebuilt and it was not until 1826 that the rubble caused by the storm was removed to make space for the present cathedral square. The Gothic tower soars 312 ft (95 m) above the town and the view from the top is worth the climb. You can pause for a rest half way up the 465 steps at St Michael's Chapel, which is fourteenth-century. At the top there is another little chapel. The cloisters are still intact and when you enter their quiet precincts you can hardly believe you are in the centre of the fourth city of Holland, where 300,000 people live.

From the far side of the cloisters you can view the Dom tower at its best and enjoy the fine flow of Gothic tracery in the vaulting covering them. From these cloisters you can enter by a door into Utrecht University, the second oldest in the country. What was once the meeting hall of the Dom is now the university auditorium. This hall witnessed the signing of a treaty in 1579 which consolidated the union of the seven Protestant provinces, out of which grew the nation of the Netherlands. This treaty was as important to the Dutch as that of the Spanish Succession was to the British. To commemorate it the stained glass windows are decorated with the coats of arms of the seven provinces. On the wall opposite the rostrum, there is a memorial to volunteer students who took part in a ten day campaign in 1830.

The rest of the auditorium walls are hung with tapestries designed by

26 *The Dom at Utrecht*

Charles de Moor and Willem van Konijnenburg, and made by The Hague Weaving School. They portray the work of the different faculties allegorically. Many of the students live in the attractive seventeenth-century houses just around the corner from the university which have been renovated recently. The university buildings include a palace built for Louis Bonaparte, King of Holland, in 1807, which is now a library; an ophthalmic institute; a natural history museum; a botanic garden, and a veterinary school.

Adrian VI, born in Utrecht, was one of the few Popes not to be an Italian. He had a house built in the capital, but died in 1523 before it was completed. Of red brick striped with white, it is still called the Pope's House. It was restored in 1959 and is used as government offices. The inner court may be visited by permission of the porter in the gatehouse.

The Oude and Nieuwe Gracht (canals) meander through Utrecht and make it the attractive town it is. On the Oude Gracht the street and quays are on different levels. Where else can you gaze from the roadway down over tree-tops onto pavements and below them again see the calm reflecting waters of canals? It is even more remarkable to realize that below the storage vaults which front the pavements are medieval cellars. People stroll up and down the flights of steps connecting the pavements and alongside the canals. Hurdy gurdies play and fruit stalls are attractively laid out to tempt passers-by on the various levels. Some of the store houses and cellars have been turned into restaurants, cafés and shops. Some cafés spill out over the pavements to the water's edge. Several cellars along a canal, suitably nicknamed 'Little Venice', have attractively arched entrances.

The quay walls sometimes have niches holding small statues. One reach, called The Crescent, is edged with small seventeenth-century houses which are entered by little bridges. These doll-like dwellings once belonged to the church. I was fortunate enough to be shown over one. The narrow white-walled hallway had green skirting boards and door frames and to the right was the drawing room, again long and narrow. As in the case of all seventeeth-century houses in Holland, large or small, the design was elongated into surprising depth. The thrifty merchants all built their houses the same way because tax depended on the width of the frontage. The drawing room windows extended the full width of the room. A steep staircase led to the next floor with a study, bedroom and bathroom, and the floor above had two more bedrooms. Most interesting of all was the cellar. Steps go down to it from the ground floor. It was dry and airy but dark until a door was opened giving onto the canal.

'A journey along the canal at sunset would be delightful and would also show the layout of the city' I remarked to our guide. She laughed. 'You must not think you are always surrounded by water here. To the east of the city we have a triple avenue of lime trees known as the Mall, and wait until you see modern Utrecht. You may wonder why we have so few statues here. The plinth in the main square is empty only because we have not found a suitable one to place there! But you must see the charming one of Anne Frank.'

The statue is charming indeed, a small figure by Pieter d'Hont in Jankerskhof. The little girl who showed such courage and remarkable endurance has her hands clasped behind her back. She wears a simple blouse and skirt and looks straight in front of her, feet firmly planted on the ground, a little apart as if, having been closed off from the outside world for so long, she cannot believe she is in the open air and sunshine. It is a touching sight but unfortunately is being moved to a new site.

Another Utrecht statue which has somewhat the same quality without the pathos is that of St Martin near the Tolsteerburg on Oude Gracht. St Martin, a Roman officer stationed in Amiens in AD 332, sits astride his horse. His cloak is turned back over his shoulder and his headdress is surmounted by a cross. The saint has had many churches named after him, one of the most famous being in London's Trafalgar Square. He is the patron saint of Utrecht. After leaving the army he entered the Church and eventually became Bishop of Tours. Like St Wenceslas, an incident which happened during bitter winter weather is that most remembered and was the reason he became converted to Christianity. He met a poorly-clad sick man in a blizzard and, filled with pity at his shivering plight, gave him half his clothing. That night Martin had a dream. He saw Christ wearing half a robe saying to the angels 'Do you know who has clothed me like this? It was Martin, so far not baptized, who protected me from the cold.' Martin was 22 years old when he saw this vision and, as was the case with St Paul, was immediately converted. The Utrecht coat of arms symbolizes this story. The red field is the clothing given by the Saint and white represents a bishop's robe.

It was in Utrecht, seat of the first Christian church in Holland, that Christianity began and spread through the Netherlands, Denmark and Norway. On Utrecht university's 300th anniversary in 1936 the Danes presented a plaque to commemorate the conversion of their people to Christianity in AD 960. It is inscribed in runic characters and reads:

> King Harald ordered this memorial to be made to commemorate his father Gorm and his mother Thyre. Harald conquered the whole of Denmark and converted the Danes and Norwegians to Christianity.

Utrecht's old fishmarket, which used to be on a canal bridge, is now a café and is a very popular place. Chairs and tables dot the bridge and you can look down along Little Venice, or across at a street bordered with enticing shops, one of which is a bakery. The smell of freshly baked bread is heady, seeping out of the doorway. All kinds of bread are there for the buying, from dense pumpernickel to light as air croissants. In the centre of a window, overflowing with buns of all shapes and sizes, stands a magnificent bread chariot dated 1762.

Holiday Inn

In Jarbeursplein the ultra-modern Holiday Inn hotel, with its 250 rooms and extensive conference facilities, vies in height with the Dom, as does its neighbour, the Hoog Catherijne, the largest shopping complex in Holland. If you have a drink in the Railroad Bar on the twenty-first floor you must sit by a window and watch what is going on below you. Little yellow trains move constantly along the rail tracks, just like a child's model railway. You are looking down on a major rail junction which has regular services to the European capitals as well as to all the Dutch cities. People on platforms and stairways are mere dots as they move to the trains or into the Hoog Catherijne complex to shop. Its main concourse is one level above ground, built above part of the rail tracks and extending several city blocks. There are a number of escalators leading up to it and all the routes are well marked. Bulk goods can be brought in at ground level and introduced into the shops above without creating a traffic problem.

Hoog Catherijne provides a quick pedestrian connection from the Industries Fair building via the Central Station to the old city centre. The station contains two bus terminals for local and intercity routes. The complex offers living accommodation in flats in three different sections. There are nine office blocks which, with the shops, give employment to 10,000 people. The Congress Centre of the Industries Fair, the Mirliton theatre and four cinemas are also there and, in complete contrast to all this, the chapel of the 'Sisters of Love' – a Silence Centre. Certainly if you want to do business or sightsee in a hurry the Holiday Inn is a good place to stay.

Museums

The Central Museum in Agnietenstraat has a section on city history with a Viking ship dating back to AD 800, paintings of the sixteenth-century Utrecht school, period rooms, sculptures, porcelain and even a doll's house made in 1680. There is an Historic Museum housed in the old Town Hall. On the top floor it has a permanent exhibition of hoop making.

In Het Catherijne Convent, or State Museum, in Nieuwegracht, the history of Christianity in the Netherlands is illustrated with an extensive collection of religious art consisting of paintings, sculptures, church vestments, manuscripts, ornaments etc. It houses the largest collection of medieval art in Holland.

The University Museum in Biltstraat has a major collection of antique instruments used in natural and medical science, including microscopes, electric machines and air pumps. Portraits, photographs, costumes and other objects give a picture of the history of the university and of student life.

The Historical Costume Museum contains ancient costumes, accessories and fabrics from the early eighteenth century to the present day, both of Western and other origin. The most unusual museum must be the one called 'From Music Box to Barrel Organ' at 38 Lange Nieuwestraat. It has a wide selection of musical curiosities ranging from small clocks to giant barrel organs. Instruments with dulcet tones vie with others whose sound is deafening. Beautifully carved and ornamented pieces stand next to gaudily painted ones. It is open all the year, except on national holidays, and sometimes there are evening recitals.

Every year the VVV in Utrecht organizes the Utrecht Mill Day in cooperation with the Foundation of the Utrecht Mill and the Guild of the Voluntary Miller. This takes place in September. Two different routes are marked out: for cars 50 miles (80 km) and for bicycles 22 miles (35 km). They pass a large number of mills several of which are open to the public. Festivities are arranged at the start and finish.

Castles and palaces

As on the outskirts of so many Dutch cities, Utrecht has its share of ancient castles scattered along the old river course, the Kromme Rhine. One is the castle de Haar 4 miles (6 km) west of Haarzuilens, built during the fifteenth century, but razed to the ground by fire in the last century. However it was rebuilt in 1892 by the architect Cuypens. It is surrounded by an attractive park – which necessitated a whole village being torn down – but the result is not unlike the gardens at Versailles. Here you can see Gobelin tapestries, Persian rugs, fragile Chinese vases and Spanish paintings. Another French connection is that you can see an engaging small carriage in which Louis XIV, the Sun King, rode as a child.

Near Baarn, at Soestdijk, the Queen Mother has a palace which was furnished by the Dutch people as a wedding gift to her. The castle, skirted by flower beds and lawns, is long and low with two colonnaded wings. A sweep of steps leads to the central doorway. The palace is painted white, and stands only a short distance back from the main road. Nearby in charming woodland Queen Beatrix and Prince Claus often stay in the seventeenth-century castle of Drakestein at Lage Vuursche.

One of the most visited places, about 11 miles (18 km) east of Utrecht, is the ivy-covered mansion at Doorn which was the Kaiser's last home. He lived in this quiet retreat (called the House of Doorn) for 21 years. It is surrounded by a water-filled moat on which swans glide silently. There are many treasures to be seen at Doorn, including one of the world's finest snuff box collections, begun by Frederick the Great. The Kaiser, who died in 1941, is buried in a redbrick mausoleum close by the house. Visitors can also see the small graves of his five dogs, his companions in exile, Wai-Wai, Arno, Senta, Topsy and Bambi.

Amersfoort

The 12 mile (19 km) drive from Utrecht to Amersfoort, the second largest town in the province, is full of delightful surprises. You leave along Maliebaan street, which has a wide green verge planted with trees, where, it is said, *Kolf,* the forerunner of golf, was played 300 years ago by university students. The woodlands behind the trees are full of deer and wild game. The land here is high above sea level and the forests have been established for centuries.

Amersfoort, encircled by a double ring of moats and ancient walls, has great medieval charm. Much of it has not altered since the twelfth century. People still live in houses built into, or on, the city walls, as in Medina in Malta. It would not be Holland without canals and a deep one flows right through the centre of the city guarded at either end by huge water gates. Although the town now spills out far beyond the walls into modern districts, once within the sturdy ramparts you forget this and the past comes to life. This is especially so during five weeks from the end of June, when every Friday morning trumpeters in medieval costume parade round the walls. These young men are borrowed trumpeters from the local garrison.

In the inner ring of houses a thirteenth-century building known as the Stump Tower stands out. It is now the Dutch Carillon School. There are other towers and steeples within the walls (which jut above the fortifications) so that from the air the old city looks like a wedding cake.

Spakenburg

On from Amersfoort you can drive through the *polders* to the fishing port of Spakenburg. Although it is a 'costume' village the women's clothes are far from pretty, even if there is a great variety of colour and pattern. The skirts are long and black and the bodice looks more like a lifejacket than anything else. It is put on like one and does up at the back. It is rigidly starched, tight across the front and sticks out over the shoulders. The community is a strict one and the families intermarry. One of the reasons given for the strange bodices is that the women are not permitted to show the shape of their breasts.

It was a sunny afternoon in December when I visited Spakenburg and bitterly cold. The canals were frozen and covered with skaters. Boys darted forwards heads down, hands clasped behind their backs. Women and girls skated in their strange costumes, their billowing skirts like sails. Sledges were pulled by laughing children. The cheeks of the skaters were rosy with their exertions. Gaily coloured washing hung right across streets frozen solid. Green house plants crowded the windows of the houses. It might have been a winter scene painted by Avercamp. All that was missing were horses and sleighs. Quite unnerving was the sight of women shoppers riding bicycles, unperturbed by the slippery surface and not getting their long skirts caught in the wheels. They must either be impervious to cold, or wear thick underwear, since none wore a coat.

The harbour protrudes right into the centre of the village. Fishing boat trips, water sports and angling are the favourite summer pastimes. Fish curing has been carried on for many years and Spakenburg smoked eel is a great delicacy.

The Saturday afternoon market is always crowded and a haunt for photographers for, although Spakenburg people have many religious scruples, they do not object to being photographed, unlike those in Staphorst. There is a quaint café at 14-18 Havenstraat which is attached to a shop full of souvenirs from costumes to china. Above the café the proprietor has furnished a room in old world Spakenburg style. Wax figures are dressed in local costumes. One of a man sits mending a net; while a boy in a high chair looks down at his small brother in a cradle. By an inlaid cupboard there are bunks let into the walls and concealed by curtains. The walls and fireplace are tiled. The family bible, with shining brass fittings, lies on a table and a framed *petit point* sampler hangs on the wall. The tables particular to this village are painted red, white and green.

I discussed the local costumes with the café owner and he told me that during the tourist season there is an exhibition of them showing how the designs were developed.

We drove back to Utrecht following the dyke along the Eemeer at sunset. Black tree trunks were silhouetted against a pink and gold sky and youngsters were still skating along the canals and ditches, their breath hanging in the still frosty air like smoke rings. We crossed the Eem by a little ferry which could only accommodate one car and does not work on Sundays! The sky darkened as we drew close to Baarn and by the time we passed by the palace of Queen Juliana it was night and all that could be seen of Soestdijk were brightly-lit windows.

7
ROTTERDAM
AND THE
PROVINCE OF ZEELAND

Rotterdam

One of the fascinating things about a small country like Holland is that there is no great distance between any of the big towns. Rotterdam is a mere 9 miles (14 km) south of The Hague. A cliché has it that The Hague governs, Amsterdam plays and Rotterdam works. The latter is true but Rotterdam's zeal has paid off. When you comprehend the scale of the rebuilding after the devastation of the Second World War, perhaps another saying has some truth. It is claimed that the Rotterdamers buy their shirts with the sleeves already rolled up; but they certainly find time to play as well.

Centuries ago, some 20 miles (32 km) inland from the sandbank that years later became the Hook of Holland, a stream named the Rotte emptied into the Rhine. The Rotte was dammed and so gave its name to a triangular fishing village which eventually grew into the world's busiest port. In 1229 John I, Count of Holland, granted it rights in the same way as Haarlem. Due to its position at the mouths of the Rhine and Maas it has always had great potential and by 1600 had become the second commercially important city in the country. The New Waterway connecting it to the Hook of Holland was started in 1869 and the town became accessible to large ships. In 1910 the port was used by 147 sailing and 9221 steam vessels. Due to its key position with Central Europe and the North Sea it continued its growth, until the German bombardment in 1940.

Visiting Rotterdam today you would not know that on 14 May 1940, Nazi bombers obliterated the centre of the city. Incendiary bombs rained down, flames enveloped everything and countless citizens died. Four years later, when the Allies landed in Normandy, German army demolition squads blew up the entire harbour installation so that nothing was left except water and ashes. Memories of the holocaust are brought back by Zadkine's statue called 'Destroyed City'. It is of a large surrealistic bronze figure with a jagged hole where its heart should be, a pain-wracked face with open mouth, and arms lifted to the sky as if to ward off more danger.

This despairing figure is in contrast to the calm statue of Erasmus in the old town square behind the Laurenskerke, a beautiful Gothic cathedral. He was born in Rotterdam on 28 October 1467. The statue was erected in 1622. He stands there quietly, his long cloak hanging in folds about his feet, reading a great book. Children are told that when the cathedral clock strikes the hour he turns a page of his book. Unbelievably, the figure of Erasmus survived the incendiary bombs of 14 May. When demolition squads removed the debris the sage kept reading his book quite unconcernedly amidst the rubble. It was a sign of hope, and the statue was removed and put in a place of safety until the war ended.

27 *The statue 'Destroyed City' in Rotterdam*

28 *The statue of Erasmus, which survived the bombing of 1940, in Rotterdam*

Erasmus
Erasmus hated everything that savoured of fanaticism or extremism and
was unquestionably the intellectual leader of his day. He travelled widely
and wrote constantly. Of illegitimate birth, as a youth he entered the
order of the Brethren of the Common Life. He became secretary to the
Bishop of Cambrai and continued his studies at the College Montaigne in
Paris. Lord Montague, one of his pupils, persuaded him to visit England,
where he studied Greek at Oxford and began his famous friendship with
Sir Thomas Moore. He was constantly on the move: in Paris, Orleans,
back to his own country, Switzerland and England, and his pen never
rested.

The Peace Palace at The Hague

The Five Flies Restaurant

Canal illuminations in Amsterdam

Adages, a collection of scattered sayings culled from classic authors, was to be one of Erasmus' most popular works and many of the sayings he quoted are still used by us today – 'Call a spade a spade', 'As plain as the nose on your face', 'One swallow does not make a spring', and others.

In Italy he was fêted, and the Venetian publisher and printer Aldus Manutius undertook to do work for him. He was tutor for a time to Alexander Stewart, the natural son of James VI of Scotland, and was professor of Greek at Cambridge. When crossing the Alps he planned *The Praise of Folly*, published in 1509, an oration delivered by Folly to an imaginary audience of all sorts and conditions of men. He wrote bitter satires against the ignorance and vice of the Catholic clergy and at the same time was scathing of Luther.

He received gifts varying from a sizable sum from Pope Clement VII to a box of sweetmeats from some nuns. He hated the sea, but enjoyed English life and so had to face the Channel time and time again. His likes and dislikes were many and often strange. White wines and beer did not suit him; he could only enjoy the wines of Burgundy. He could not eat or abide the smell of fish. He would say that his heart was Catholic but his stomach was Lutheran. Of his work, his Greek Testament caused perhaps the greatest stir and its impact on opinion was durable and profound. No doubt his enemies were many, but few could ignore him. He steered a middle course and had no desire to be a martyr, but rather laboured to make people think.

Statues

Sculptured figures play a great part in the layout of the new Rotterdam. A girl seated in a chair looks over at the Doelen Concert Hall. Perhaps she hears music from the copper-roofed building or is musing upon its vastness. In the Crooswijk cemetery there is a statue of a kneeling woman with a dove on one arm. At her feet there is a casket containing a scroll with the names of the victims who could be identified after the Rotterdam air raid. Beside the many statues on display, others have been bought and stored for future use in new squares and parks. However, the one of Erasmus is as much a part of Rotterdam as the port. His house, which was kept as a museum, was destroyed in the air raid of May 1940, but his statue seems indestructible and it is amusing to watch small boys glancing up at his thin ascetic figure when the clock strikes, half fearful that he really will turn the page. In 1969, an Erasmus stamp was issued by the Dutch Post Office commemorating his birth 500 years earlier. It was designed by S. L. Hartz in Haarlem and issued on 30 September. Rotterdam's University also remembers its humanist philosopher by using his name.

New architecture

Rotterdam's phoenix-like rise from its ashes has produced some imaginative architecture and some of the new buildings are well worth examination, such as The Beehive department store, devoid of windows and with outside walls of round indentations like a honeycomb, or the 24 storey Shell building (originally meant to look like a giant petrol pump, but fortunately the design was rejected) which appears to consist entirely of windows.

Should you arrive by train you will come out of the station into Stationsplein, bounded on one side by Weena. The harbour is to the south and between the two lies the central core of the city. Opposite you is the Bouwcentrum, a type of museum with exhibits of lighting, heating and different building structures. It has a library, and there are training courses for engineers, town planners and architects. Across the Weena, to the left, runs the Lijnbaan, a shopping and leisure centre closed to traffic, and the Rotterdam Hilton hotel. Behind the station to the far right you will find the Royal Rotterdam Zoo which is open until sunset. It allows animals to live in surroundings that are as natural as possible, and there are lakes, meadows and high cliffs. It is called the Blijdorp – Happy Village. The reptile house and fresh and sea water aquariums are captivating.

The Lijnbaan   This large shopping complex is suitably named after a businessman's dream of 1667. He built a covered rope walk in the town centre of that day and now, 300 years later, over the same ground there is a new Lijnbaan. Spacious arcaded precincts edged by shops are prohibited to motorists. There are flower beds, trees, fountains, statues and even aviaries. Shoppers can rest and have drinks or coffee in small plazas, and at weekends there are concerts and pop music in the squares. Even bicycles are banned, unusual in Holland, so there is a free and easy atmosphere for strollers.

Near the Lijnbaan shopping centre is Coolsingel, where nearly all the buildings are post-war, with the exception of the Town Hall and the Schielandhuis Museum. Rotterdam's western district is quite different from the modern part of the city. Delftshaven, which before its absorption in 1886 was the harbour of Delft, is a maze of narrow streets and waterways. A magnet for Americans, many of the buildings have been restored as they were in 1620. These belonged to Pilgrim families who lived there before boarding the *Speedwell*, the ship which set sail for England and thence crossed the Atlantic to America. The Pilgrim Fathers' church is open to the public, as is the Sack Carriers House which was built in 1653. It used to be a place where workers called and waited to be selected for jobs, many in vain. However hope lifted hearts because everyone had a chance by throwing dice to see who would be the lucky ones to be selected.

An interesting place to visit for more than one reason is Schiedam. This is to the west of the city and there are 50 gin distilleries there including that of Bols. Sampling can be reviving on a cold day! At Melchers, 74 Lange Haven, there is the De Jongh collection of some 5000 miniature bottles. It has taken half a century to accumulate them, representing well known and unheard of brands from many different countries.

De Doelen   Close by the Lijnbaan is De Doelen, Rotterdam's music and concert hall. Opened in May 1966 at a cost of $9 million it is said to have flawless acoustics. Two quaint hexagonal penthouses are auditoriums, one accommodating 600 people, the other over 2000. Seating consists of foam rubber armchairs and both halls are fitted with simultaneous translation equipment. This strange building can function as congress centre or concert hall and has several small theatres.

Hilton Hotel   The Hilton faces the large fountain in the middle of the Hofplein where Weena and Coolsingel meet, but its main entrance is at the back. It is the city's most luxurious hotel with several restaurants and 254 rooms. It has recently been refurbished. The Le Jardin restaurant has been redecorated and can also function as a meeting room for parties for 150 to 500 guests. The Golden Ballroom and four smaller rooms have been converted into an elegant casino. The decor is in pastel shades, with touches of red breaking the traditional practice. It offers French and American roulette, baccarat and black jack. Modern surveillance equipment is installed in the ceiling overlooking the tables. A separate area has gambling machines. Access is from the street or the hotel. There is strict control to ensure that young people under the age of 18 do not enter and all guests are obliged to show some form of identification. Visitors must adhere to the worldwide casino rules regarding dress, with gentlemen wearing jackets and tie (available on loan from the reception desk). Problems can occur determining what is correct attire for ladies, who can look chic in simple jeans.

Being the only *de luxe* hotel in Rotterdam, many famous people stay here. Some wish the public to know, others like to remain incognito. Pop stars love it because the hotel staff are very discreet. The Rolling Stones stayed for several weeks and no one knew. Emirs and sheiks from the Arab States find their desire for privacy respected; those seeking medical aid and wishing to remain anonymous often stay. Rotterdam has acquired a great reputation in those circles for eye treatment.

Museums

The Boymans — van Beuningen Museum   This is one of the Netherlands' best endowed museums, principally because it houses the incredible private collection of an oil magnate, the late van Beuningen. The exhibits include many major works by Frans Hals, Rembrandt, van Gogh, van Eyck, Bosch and Rubens. A personal favourite of van Beuningen was Peter Breughel's *Tower of Babel* which he enjoyed contemplating and his reward lay in constantly finding new details. One of the most charming Rembrandts is a portrait of his son Titus.

Maritime Museum   This museum is a rewarding one for visitors and has the authentic nautical atmosphere from being housed offshore in the ship *De Buffel*, an old ironclad of 1868.

City tours

An unexpected way of seeing the city is a tour by tram. When I did this an ancient vehicle was in use which made so much noise that the multilingual commentary was inaudible. It is to be replaced by a modern tram like those which operate on the city routes, or possibly by a coach, which would be a pity. The frequent pauses while the driver or commentator steps down with a large crowbar and throws the points, provide natural opportunities during which you can look around.

Rotterdam has the first Metro transit system to be built in Holland. Some of it is above ground while other parts run in underground tubes, the waterproofing of which presented a problem in this low-lying city, especially where it passes beneath the Maas. The trains are fitted with the latest automatic safety features which apply the brakes if a driver ignores a warning signal for more than two seconds. The stations are marked with a large illuminated M, and my husband gained the impression that MacDonalds Hamburgers were having great success in Rotterdam until he learned to distinguish between the two signs. Further evidence of improved communication is the installation of a fibre optic phone cable ring round the city. This will shortly give digital connection via satellites to anywhere in the world.

Visitors to Copenhagen are quick to recognize the Bourse by its steeple of entwined dragons' tails. In Rotterdam distinctive buildings are just as easy to find. Some have been given nicknames such as the Pencil, the Wedge of Cake, the Dunce's Cap – an apartment block – and the Aerofoil, which is eventually to form part of the world trade centre. There is also the Paper Clip which looks as if it was made of giant paper clips and is faced with multicoloured tiles.

'Tree homes'

Perhaps the most controversial type of home in Rotterdam is the brain child of Piet Blom, and there are several of them linked together. They cause such a stir when first put up that even architectural circles could not agree upon a simple name to describe them, so they have ended up with three – tree, cube and pillar. They stand over some roads in a line like tilted sugar cubes at odd angles on pillars. Piet Blom prefers the label 'Tree Home'. Here is his own description of them and how he came to design them.

> I had to create a pedestrian route from the city's main market and the Central Library to the Old Harbour area. I did not believe that anyone would use the bridge unless I put destinations on it which people would go to for their own sake. I used the Rialto Bridge in Venice and the old London Bridge as examples, but I had to solve the additional problem of a high noise level both from the road and from passing trains. I turned the top room with its many windows into a kind of conservatory for pot plants to compensate for the lack of a balcony. If you look at the houses in a row you can see I have used a classic architectural theme. Essentially it is a basilica, a vaulted structure, which has been used in Christianity for at least 1500 years. All basilicas are really imitations of a line of trees.

29 *Piet Blom's 'tree houses'*

Whatever people thought about the architecture his 38 houses were sold six months before they were completed. They are so extraordinary in shape that onlookers not only wished to see them but also to venture inside. One owner decided to open his cube home for a small fee to the curious. Many visitors felt dizzy just looking at radiators placed at 45 degree angles, sloping floors and tilted walls. The hanging of curtains and pictures seemed to be impossible. Whatever the visitors thought, and however the owner solved his problems, money poured in from about 35,000 visitors within five months.

Rotterdam Town Hall miraculously survived destruction during the war and is one of the largest in Holland. Built on 8000 concrete piles in 1920, it is an attractive place and the city War Memorial stands in front of it.

There are two types of visitors to Rotterdam from Britain – business people and tourists. The businessman or woman, used to wasting time at airports, finds it convenient to fly by the Tulip Express, which operates three times daily between Gatwick and Rotterdam. Check-in times and formalities are kept to a minimum, because of quick customs control at both airports. Tourists find that Rotterdam is conveniently placed for most of the sightseeing destinations. It has two things to offer, the ultra-modern city and the world's largest harbour.

Shipping

Rotterdam has been called a 'harbour with a city attached' and this is true. Certainly there are two tours which you must make: one around the city and the other of the harbour. The city tour options are best discussed with the VVV at the station. As for the harbour, Spido (the company which offers the sightseeing boats) have a number of vessels which start from Willemsplein every 45 minutes. The route and commentary are excellent and give a dramatic impression of the port. Everything is gigantic: dry docks, shipyards, cranes, oil tankers and container ships. Most containers are handled by the specialized quays and cranes, but some are off-loaded onto smaller barges which can take them directly into the inland waterways. Astride the Rhine and Maas rivers and close to the North Sea, it can accommodate the largest tankers and shipping of any size, for its main entrance has been deepened. The rivers link it with Germany, Switzerland, Belgium and France.

The quays now stretch more than 23 miles (37 km) to the North Sea and land reclamation has created a new industrial region in the interland. By night, at Parnis across the water, the largest oil refining complex on the continent reddens the sky for miles with its candlelike torches. The river traffic is so interesting and there is so much to see that you no sooner seem to step aboard your cruiser than you are back at the landing stage again; but then you can always repeat the trip.

All shipping movement is controlled by radar and arrivals and departures seem to be continuous. Endless lines of barges are towed into the Maas, bound for Germany. Floating cranes like huge ostriches raise and lower their necks depositing loads into ships' holds.

The Euromast

Over everything towers the slender Euromast, Rotterdam's trademark. Its lower section is 340 ft (104 m) high, with two restaurants close to the top. If you wish to venture even higher, you can step into a lift which encircles the upper part of the tower, as a nut surrounds a bolt. It rotates as it moves up and down, taking you to and from the Space Tower, 600 ft (183 m) above ground. The panorama on a clear day is unsurpassed. There are two glass-enclosed restaurants, one self-service offering a wide choice of food and the Rotisserie where you can eat *à la carte* while enjoying the fabulous view. If you make a reservation you can even have breakfast. You may wonder why the restaurants do not rotate as do similar ones in America and Canada. When you take your seat at table you will find the answer. Here the scenery itself in the great waterway below moves around you instead.

Zeeland

An interesting excursion from Rotterdam is to drive south to Zeeland to see one of the greatest engineering projects the Dutch have ever tackled – the Delta works. It has been under construction for a quarter of a century and the last stage is now under way, the building of a movable marine flood gate across the estuary of the Oosterschelde River. It is the first of its kind ever attempted. There is an information centre where you can view a model of the venture. It is designed to protect south-west Holland from any further flood disasters like the flood that occurred in 1953. At that time a storm of unprecedented velocity struck the coast at the same time as the spring flood tide. Water poured over the dykes, undermining them so that they gave way. The sea swept over almost the whole province. It even edged into the streets of Rotterdam and lapped against the cathedral walls of Dordrecht. It was the worst disaster in the province since the Second World War.

Walcheren, which juts into the sea at the mouth of the river Schelde, at that time had been fortified by the Nazis, and the Allies had to breach the dykes to flush out the Germans. Nearly all of Walcheren disappeared beneath the incoming water, leaving a wilderness of mud in which not a tree or shrub survived except on higher ground. It was a heavy price to pay to open the way to the great port of Antwerp, but it had to be done and the Dutch were stoical about it. You can still see reminders of those days at Westkapelle, facing the Schelde, where old gun emplacements bear the marks of shelling by British warships. A stone tablet recalls the episode in Dutch and English with a brief sentence: 'The 4th Commando Brigade British Liberation Army landed here November 1st 1944 to liberate the island'. Few other traces remain and Walcheren is again the garden of Zeeland, its fields green and fertile, the towns and villages brighter and fresher than ever before. Though it is now joined to the mainland, Vlissingen, the cross Channel terminal on its tip is some 60 miles (96 km), mostly motorway, from Rotterdam. It could be described as a rectangular dish jutting into the sea at the most westerly point of Holland, the rim being the high sand dunes and dykes which keep out the sea.

Vlissingen

There are only three towns, Vlissingen, Middleburg and Goes. Vlissingen is a fishing and ship-building centre. Its promenade has been successively named after well-known sea captains, De Ruyter, Bankert and now Evertsen. Inland lies Bellamy Park where flowerbeds surround a bust of J. Bellamy, a native poet. Then there is the Stedelijk Museum full of local antiquities. It is a picturesque town where, it is said, you 'wake up unconscious' due to the heady sea air. From Vlissingen a ferry crosses the mouth of the Westerschelde to Breskens which is still Dutch territory, but only some 20 miles (32 km) from Ghent in Belgium. Bruges, Antwerp and Brussels are also within easy reach, all of them cities which are well worth a visit.

Middleburg

Middleburg, the provincial capital, is a busy, attractive town. Many of its lovely old buildings survived the wartime bombing, but meticulous attention to detail has been paid to the restoration of the damaged ones. Lange Jan, the historic abbey and the Town Hall are excellent examples. Many handsome merchants' houses and warehouses escaped destruction and you may still see the Gistpoort (1509). The Kuiperspoort (Coopers Guild) area is more photographed than most sights in this photogenic town. Some of the old warehouses have been converted into a music school.

The Town Hall facing the main square is one of Holland's most attractive, with a spacious reception hall furnished with antiques and Old Master paintings. The Vleeshal (meat market) behind is a museum housing a model of the island under water in 1944. There is much to admire here and it is a prime example of a picturesque maritime town which has preserved its old beauty. Though 1100 houses are protected, the construction of new buildings is encouraged. There are bright

30 *The Tower of St Lieven Monster Church at Middleburgh*

shopping centres and modern facilities. If you want to see it at its liveliest go there on a Thursday when they hold the butter market in the main square. There are the usual stalls selling everything except butter. Tourists mingle with villagers from all over Walcheren, many wearing their distinctive traditional dresses of long black skirts, floral aprons and white headdresses in lace with golden side ornaments.

The city also has a miniature representation of Walcheren, reminiscent of Madurodam near The Hague. It is open from Easter to September and covers about 8000 sq. yd (6700 sq. m) with harbours, roads, dykes, villages and their surroundings, all to one-twentieth scale. Some 200 buildings nestle among 120,000 dwarf trees and shrubs and there are tiny dredgers, ships and cranes all working busily. When darkness falls, thousands of lights come on. You are even shown a re-enactment of the epic flooding of the island during the war and its miraculous rebirth.

Veere

A few miles from Middleburg is lovely and historic Veere – more a village than a town. Yet 500 years ago it was one of the best known ports in Europe rivalling Bruges and Antwerp. It was owned by the powerful van Borsselen family who had marriage links with the Scottish Royal Family. It was natural, therefore, that it should become the port for Scottish wool, a valuable monopoly. Thus began the intriguing connection with Scotland which resulted in a Scots colony with their own Conservator (a mixture of company president, local judge and Scottish ambassador). They were given several houses and warehouses and two of the finest, dating from 1539, remain today – stone-faced mansions on the tree-fringed quayside. One is called de Struys (The Ostrich), the other Het Lammekin (The Little Lamb). The two houses are now a museum containing old maps, costumes, ironwork and china, while the cellars have been converted into a restaurant. One of the treasures can be seen in a glass case. It is the original 'Proclamation for Reestablishing the Staple Port at Camphire' (Scots spelling of the old Campveer). The signature is King William's, the date 30 March 1669.

There are many other delightful sixteenth-century houses on the quay and at the far end in Campveerse Toren, a round tower which once guarded the harbour entrance. It is now a small hotel and restaurant. There is a view over the Veerse Meer, the lake formed when the dam shut out the sea in 1961. When this was built the days of Veere as a harbour ended. It has long ceased to have any maritime importance, but fishing boats had succeeded the galleons of old. Then they, too, departed to be followed by today's glossy yachts, whose world is the water sports area of the Veerse Meer. Only the vast empty church which was never finished, the lovely Town Hall with its slim soaring tower and old houses remain to recall the past glories.

Walcheren

Walcheren is easy to reach whether by car, coach or bicycle, and it is quite small with all its towns and villages quite close together. Domberg is the principal seaside resort, a charming little village which has never forgotten that Carmen Silva, Queen of Romania, once stayed there. Her

31 *The Town Hall at Veere*

villa is now a pension. There are several other modest resorts round the
coast with plenty of self-catering accommodation and campsites. As
always the VVV will help you. Many spotless little houses offer bed and
breakfast in the summer. The best hotel is the Zuiderduin at Westkapelle
which belongs to the Golden Tulip chain.

Fishing

Zeeland is a paradise along its coastline for fishermen. There are many species: mackerel, plaice, flounder, sole, seapike, bass, trout, eel and cod. In the offshore waters fishing is generally unrestricted but licences are necessary for inland waters. Fully outfitted fishing boats sail every day from 15 of Zeeland's harbours in summer and winter.

8

GELDERLAND

Arnhem

The capital of Gelderland is Arnhem, probably one of the best-known names in Holland to those abroad because of the Allies' airborne attack on the Germans which had such tragic results during the last war. Edging the right bank of the Rhine it acts as a crossroads for Holland, Belgium and Germany. The Dutch describe it in an erudite way as a hand with fingers spread. The palm is the city centre with hotels, restaurants, outdoor cafés, shopping centre and market square. The fingers are the green suburbs, built against the Veluwezoom hills. Between the fingers are the city parks. These are not enclosed by the town but lead out to the countryside. This green belt shows how far-sighted the local council was many years ago when they gradually bought up eight large estates as they came on the market.

32 *A dyke in Gelderland*

Provincial House

The branch of the Rhine at Arnhem is narrow. The old County Council building, near the famous bridge for which the Allies lost so many lives, was completely destroyed except for the north gate during the fighting. It has been rebuilt in ultra-modern style and linked to the old gate by an overhead glass tunnel. It symbolizes Arnhem today, and if you take a tour through it, you will understand the people better. Apart from aiming at beauty and modern efficiency the architect, J. J. M. Vegter, wished to create a place where the heart of the province pulsates.

Beneath a phoenix on the walls of the entrance gate there is the following inscription:

DEVASTATA MCMXLIV. Brought down by earthly forces.
RENOVATA MCMLIV. What God restores has greater strength.

The ground floor is as dark as a grotto, with a sculpted fountain of sirens dancing around Odysseus. A broad stairway leads up to the south gallery where light pours in through a continuous line of windows reaching from floor to ceiling and facing the Rhine. In true Dutch style great urns of tastefully arranged flowers and plants stand in front of the long expanse of glass at regular intervals. The ceiling is of slatted mahogany which cuts the glare from the light on sunny days.

The Provincial States Meeting Room has walls of glazed brick in black and white. The gilded furniture is embossed with coats of arms. The thick grey carpet has been designed with a map of Gelderland, and near the east wall a bust of the Queen Mother stands on a plinth. The chandeliers, a gift from the Electricity Board, are gilded shafts tipped with shell-shaped bulbs. There are boxes for the public, and a press gallery.

In the Queen's Commissioners room, where the walls are covered in scrolled white linen, there is an open fire place which is sometimes used. The decoration above this represents the Fates. The focal point in the room of the Chief Clerk is a 150-year-old grandfather clock. The walls are panelled. Four tapestries in the north gallery represent the four elements: earth, air, fire and water. Beneath these are the words 'to be, to come into being, to do, to know – the four activites of man'. The corridors have long benches covered in cow skins on which people can rest.

From the galleries and corridors you can look down into a large enclosed courtyard. The fountain in one corner was designed by Professor Esser and shows the figures of Hercules and Antaeus. Beneath the windows in this courtyard the walls are sculpted with scenes from the battle of Arnhem in 1944.

If you pass through the glass corridor to the old gate, whose two cone-shaped towers look like wimples, you find yourself in a different age.

You enter a charming old-fashioned room by opening a heavy wooden door decorated with brass nailheads. The walls are lined with hundreds of books, many of them on provincial law. Council members often lunch here and are served from a modern kitchen which, I was told, was almost omitted (just as in the case of the Palace of Peace in The Hague).

The Provincial House was completed in 1954 and houses many memorial gifts. When the annual tattoo takes place in the square behind it, all the NATO flags are flown. The square is surrounded by impressive buildings. Opposite the Provincial House is what is called the 'Devil's House', built by a rich general many years ago. He was a pompous man and wished to have a gold staircase installed, but the council forbade it as being too ostentatious. In revenge the general had little devil masks placed along the façade and on the roof a statue of the devil himself to poke fun at everyone going by. Today the Lord Mayor has a large room on the first floor and it is a favourite place for young folk to get married.

Opposite this strange house there is the thirteenth-century church of St Nicholas. It suffered greatly during the Second World War but was restored to its original state. The senior minister objected to such ostentation, but when he found that his own statue was to be added as well he said no more, which in turn infuriated his parishioners! A nude statue representing 'Freedom' stands to one side of the church, but can scarcely be seen on Tuesdays, Fridays and Saturdays when there is a market in front of the building.

Court of Justice

The nearby Court of Justice was badly damaged in 1944 during the fighting but is now rebuilt. Stretching along the Rhine from the Provincial House the lovely old façades of the seventeenth-century houses have been restored. Alongside the modern highway near the bridge a cycle path has a memorial to those who died, in the form of a broken column. It was made from a piece of masonry taken from the old Palace of Justice when it was bombed. A splendid old palace which escaped destruction has been given by the Royal Family for old age pensioners from the services, who wear uniform in the 'Chelsea Pensioner' tradition.

The new section of Arnhem has mushroomed into a magnificent shopping centre since 1964 and has been well planned. The flats are attractive and are not only of the usual skyscraper type, but also long low buildings, almost Eastern in style, with arabesque arches. Stores include branches of the country's largest chains such as Vroom and Dreesman and the Bijenkorf and there are excellent hotels and restaurants.

Open Air Museum

Arnhem is rich in parks and on the northern side the Arnhem Open Air
Museum has been called one of the best tourist attractions in the
Netherlands. The park covers over 100 acres (40 ha) and contains
reassembled buildings from all over the country. These were taken to
pieces and reconstructed using, wherever possible, the original materials. A costume museum has one of the finest collections of regional dress
in the country, some of which are still worn today. All the buildings have
suitable surroundings under trees, alongside flower gardens and ponds,
meadows and woods. It is extraordinary how farmhouses differ from
province to province. There are windmills, green painted wooden
houses from the Zaan area, farmhouse kitchens complete with all their
equipment, parlours, bedrooms, stalls and workshops. You can wander
round a village brewery, a horse-driven oil mill or a village school, or
follow the various operations in a paper mill. Should you like a rest there
is a restaurant, an inn and a herb garden where you can relax. On every
side you will find picturesque scenes offering perfect subjects for
photography or an idyllic setting for a stroll. You can follow various
marked routes taking one, two or more hours. There is always
something going on: slide shows in the lecture hall or, in the summer,
demonstrations of old crafts.

The museum lies close to the A12/E36 (Oberhausen–Utrecht) road on
the northern edge of Arnhem. It is easy to reach from the railway station.
It is open from April to November, Tuesday to Friday, 9 a.m. to 5 p.m.,
Saturday and Sunday 10 a.m. to 5 p.m. On Mondays the museum area is
open but the buildings are closed except for exhibitions, the De
Hanekamp Inn, the souvenir shop and the car park.

National Park de Hoge Veluwe

This park lies inside a triangle formed by Arnhem, Apeldoorn and Ede.
It covers 22 sq miles (57 sq km) and has two special features. It is the
natural home of many hundreds of red deer, roebuck and wild boar, and
houses two museums; one is the hunting lodge of St Hubert (which can
be visited by appointment made by phone or letter) and the other the
famous Kröller-Müller museum. The park is open every day and offers a
large measure of freedom and quiet. The entrance fee includes access to
the Kröller-Müller museum, the Sculpture Garden and the Observation
Park, where there is a stand for observing the deer at close range. Buses
leave the centre of Arnhem every hour to visit this and other places of
interest.

The park is criss-crossed with roads, cycle tracks and footpaths, except
for the parts reserved for animals. There are free white bicycles which
anybody can use to go round the park in typical Dutch fashion. There are

woods, moorland, fens, marshes, formal gardens and a 25 acre (10 ha) Sculpture Garden with works by Marta Pan, Rodin, Hepworth, Bourdelle, Lipchitz, Moore and many other artists. The park has a restaurant called de Koperen Kop.

Originally the whole area was the property of Anton Kröller and his wife, the former Helene Müller, who was an art collector. In 1935 she gave her collection, one of the first important collections of modern art in the world, to the State, and the museum to house it was designed by the architect Henry van de Velde in 1937-8 and extended in 1975-7 by W. G. Quist. The building is one storey with huge picture windows overlooking lawns, flower beds and trees. The Kröller-Müllers wanted their museum to be built so that their collection should be seen in a beautiful setting.

The collection consists mainly of paintings, sculptures and drawings of the nineteenth and early twentieth centuries (Ensor, Toorop, Leger, Mondrian, Van der Lecke). However, it also includes paintings of the sixteenth and seventeenth centuries (including Baldung Grien, Cranach), old Chinese and ancient Greek ceramics, and jade figures from the Far East. The central feature is the splendid assemblage of 278 works by Vincent van Gogh. This is shown in the old part of the building with more paintings by Seurat, Rodin, Braque, Picasso, Juan Gris and others. One room of van Gogh shows the artist at his saddest when hope seems to have left him. He portrays poverty-stricken people in despair, several charcoal drawings of women road sweepers whose figures have no resilience, and weary farmers toiling in the fields. One charming picture is of the artist's dog, a mongrel, wistfully holding up one paw.

Following on from these subjects the artist's mood changes and there are several pictures of his life in France. One of the most famous is *The Bridge* with its vividly coloured horses and cart in the foreground. This was painted at Arles where the artist lived for some time. Another Arles subject is the local postman. He has bright blue eyes and a luxurious wavy beard and van Gogh painted him at least six times. The postman, Roulin, and his wife appear to have replaced van Gogh's own parents, who never understood him and did their best to discourage his painting. His own self-portrait with red hair and beard stares at the onlooker enquiringly with fixed blue eyes.

The new part of the museum is devoted to developments in art from about 1950 to the present day, principally sculptures and drawings (including Caro, King, Beuys, Ruckriem, Merz, Nevelson, Schoonhoven). There are sculptures on either side of the path leading to the main entrance.

Burgers zoo and safari park
Arnhem has the biggest and most unusual zoological garden in Holland.
It is located in the woods to the north of the city. The animals have been
given plenty of room to move – the wolves in their own forest section
and the chimpanzees on their own island. You can observe their family
life from a covered gallery. There are free flight aviaries and you can walk
through an enormous glass-enclosed tropical landscape with streams and
bridges. Reptiles and crocodiles gaze from the banks at you like silent
statues until they slide into the water and swim quickly away. You walk
through this huge greenhouse, in its hot steamy atmosphere, for long
enough to get quite a shock when you come outside again. Indeed
everything is so unlike an ordinary zoo that you tend to walk far more
than you realize. Should you feel tired there is a restaurant, or you can
board the safari train and have a 45-minute journey among many large
African animals. You can return along small woodland paths to a rock
structure with rhinos, tapirs and dwarf hippos.

You can walk back to the exit via the pheasant park with its
fantastically coloured birds some of which, unfortunately, have become
as rare as they are beautiful.

The zoo adjoins the safari park and you can go through it on the same
train which takes you round the zoo. However, it is more interesting to
drive through in your own car as then you can stop where you like for as
long as you please. You drive through an expanse of forest and moorland
along a winding road. The park is surrounded by a high double fence
system, one to keep the lions in and the other to keep the people out. You
enter through an electrically-operated gate which closes behind you
before the second one opens in front of you so that the animals cannot
walk out.

Once inside you could almost be on safari, and there is a breakdown
truck, decorated with zebra markings, on hand in case of trouble. As in
all game reserves, of course, you must never leave your car or even wind
down your windows. The first lion I saw was stretched out by a tree
stump some distance away. He stood up gracefully and began to come
towards the road. Although he appeared to move slowly, the length of
his body enabled him to cover a good deal of ground in a short space of
time. The feeding truck was in front of our car and he padded towards it
and was thrown a hunk of raw meat. He lay down where it landed and
took it between his front paws and sniffed it a few times to make sure it
was to his taste. He did not eat it right away but lifted his head lazily to
watch us with wide topaz eyes as we drove past him.

We kept a short distance behind the food truck to see what else would
happen. It came to a halt in a grove of trees and we stopped too. Suddenly
through the undergrowth came a string of young lionesses, scurrying

and bouncing towards the truck. The driver hurriedly threw out chunks of meat. The animals ate the food slowly and then one went towards the truck and stretched up to the driver's window so that its front paws rested on the outside ledge of the closed window. Another lioness loped towards the truck, jumped up on the bonnet and then onto the roof and, with its great paws hanging down, looked back over its shoulders at our parked car with bright yellow eyes. One could easily see why it is dangerous to open windows. When the truck driver started his engine the animals jumped off and made their way slowly back into the undergrowth.

The next group we came to were not interested in the food thrown from the truck but stayed where they were, half concealed by yellow bracken near a clump of trees. They remained perfectly still, heads turned in our direction. No doubt they would collect their food later. Mating among lions seems to be for life and they produce from two to six cubs at a time in captivity. Lions in safari parks seem to have readjusted their normally nocturnal habits to some extent and do move about and feed in daylight, which helps the camera enthusiast.

The Battle of Arnhem

Many who come to Arnhem associate the name with the battle in September 1944 when the town was torn asunder. Earlier that summer American and British forces had made their way from the Seine and liberated much of Belgium and France. By the middle of September they were ready for a further push forward and, inevitably, this meant crossing the Rhine.

The First British Airborne Division, toughened by service in Italy and North Africa and led by Major General Urquhart, together with the First Polish Independent Parachute Brigade commanded by Major General Sosabowski, were given a short explicit order. 'Capture Arnhem bridge and hold it.'

Parachutists rained from the skies where white trails criss-crossed the blue as gliders and aircraft came and went. The rest of the story is history. The unknown presence of two German tank divisions prevented the capture of the bridge and, after incredible resistance against overwhelming odds for ten days, the Allies were forced to withdraw. Such heroism was not to go unrewarded and it enabled forces at Nijmegen to capture the bridge there. Field Marshal Montgomery was to write in a letter to General Urquhart later:

> In the annals of the British Army there are glorious deeds. In our army we have always drawn great strength and inspiration from past traditions and endeavoured to live up to the high standards of those who have gone before. But there can be few episodes more glorious than the epic

of Arnhem and those that follow after will find it hard to live up to the high standard that you have set.

So long as we have in the armies of the British Empire officers and men who will do as you have done, then we can indeed look forward with complete confidence to the future.

In the years to come it will be a great thing for a man to be able to say 'I fought at Arnhem'.

Only 2000 of the 10,000 men who landed at Arnhem were able to get back to the Allied lines. Those of their comrades who were killed are buried in the Airborne Cemetery at Oosterbeek. At the entrance to the cemetery you walk along beach stone shingle through blue wrought iron gates where you are faced by a plain rectangular white stone bearing the words 'Their name liveth for evermore'. To one side of the entrance stands a small hall containing the Roll of Honour.

In September 1946 Queen Wilhelmina inaugurated the Airborne monument at Oosterbeek and each family in the village has adopted, and is responsible for, one grave in the cemetery. Oosterbeek school children lay flags on the graves every 17 September during the Remembrance Service. The valiant Dutch are not forgotten on this occasion. After the battle of Arnhem only 282 houses in the town remained habitable and the Germans, in vengeance for the heroic resistance put up by the local people, evacuated the remaining population by force and confiscated most of their belongings as war spoils.

The Airborne Museum
The Airborne Museum was founded in 1949 as a tribute to the British and Polish Airborne Troops. Until 1978 it occupied part of Doorwerth Castle, but then perfect accommodation was obtained in the former Divisional Headquarters, Hartenstein, at Oosterbeek. Major General Urquhart reopened the expanded museum on 11 May, 1978. A large model of the area with a spoken commentary has been set up. Slides and photographs with detailed captions illustrate the course of the battle. There is a large collection of original weapons and equipment, both Allied and German. Scenes of the battle are depicted in dioramas in the cellars with considerable attention to historical accuracy and detail. One shows a street scene in Oosterbeek. British troops halt on their way to the bridge to enquire of a member of the Dutch Resistance the shortest way into Arnhem. They are in a jeep towing a six pounder anti-tank gun.

Perhaps the most impressive scene portrayed in the cellars is in a low ceilinged room, with uniformed figures tensely awaiting instructions from General Urquhart. The lifelike wax figures which were made in Madame Tussaud's workshops stand round a table covered with maps. The general is about to speak. (He presented the uniform and beret that he actually wore in 1944 to the museum in 1978; the following year he added to the authenticity by donating his field glasses.)

The museum stands in a park which is open to the public. Two anti-tank guns which were used in the action stand near the house together with a Sherman tank which was left behind after the eventual liberation of Oosterbeek in April 1945.

Doorwerth Castle
This castle is situated on the Rhine between Oosterbeek and Renkum. The oldest part dates back to the thirteenth century. In the course of its history the castle has been repeatedly destroyed, rebuilt and extended. In spring 1945, after the battle of Arnhem, the building in which large quantities of German ammunition were stored was blown up.

Restoration was begun shortly after the end of the war and the castle was fully restored to its former glory by 1982, though the north and east wings are not yet open to the public. In 1974 the first and only Netherlands Hunting Museum was inaugurated in the south wing. This museum, concentrating on game and game management, provides information about the biology of game, the place of hunting in modern society and the history of hunting in the Low Countries. It is open Monday to Friday 10 a.m. to 5 p.m., Saturdays, Sundays and Public Holidays 1 p.m. to 5 p.m.

The National Sports Centre Popendal in Arnhem is of interest to sports lovers for it offers superb facilities for training and coaching. A number of foreign groups, including British, come here to train on the international size athletic track, and there are well-equipped lecture and demonstration rooms.

Arnhem is very keen on sport, and Scandinavian footballers have been coming here in recent years for intensive training in the spring when winter has scarcely subsided in their own countries. Now, other swimmers, cyclists and oarsmen are discovering the advantages of spring training in Holland.

In another unusual place in Arnhem disabled people live in a complex of buildings with shops, a supermarket, library, hairdressing salon and so on. The doctor at the local spastics hospital conceived this venture and his hospital backed him. People gave their time and money readily to make this small town within a town a success. The inhabitants all help each other and gradually the project has become self-supporting. The shops are attracting outside interest and making a good turnover. Many nurses give some of their free time, those interested in reading help in the library for so many hours a week, and it is difficult to realize that many of the helpers in this successful venture have never been formally trained.

Nijmegen

Nijmegen, a mere 12 miles (19 km) south of Arnhem, is the largest city in the province and, unusual in Holland, stands on the slopes of five hills rising from the Rhine. It can offer the same cultural activities as Arnhem. There is a theatre, and art exhibitions with some of the works on sale are held in a number of smaller galleries. It is a university town with some 15,000 students attending the Catholic University. There are several good eating places and a selection of student cafés and restaurants, suitably priced.

Nijmegen is one of the oldest towns in the Netherlands. Its history goes back some 2000 years to Roman times. Several emperors and kings have resided here, for the town is strategically placed on a bend of the river Waal.

The Valkhof (these days a delightful public park to the east of the town) was once the site of the Carolingian Emperor's palace. There are the remains of a chapel and part of the so-called Barbarossa ruin, the origins of which go back to the twelfth century when it was built by Frederic Barbarossa.

The Renaissance Town Hall was built in 1554 and is adorned with effigies of kings and emperors, who lent their patronage to the town in the old days. Its interior echoes the past with tapestries, pictures, fine wood carvings and a cumbersome ancient safe. A story goes that the town charters, which were kept in it, were so jealously guarded that, whenever they were taken out, the city gates were closed and the local garrison put on alert. The square tower of St Stephen's Groote Kerk is a feature of the skyline. This attractive border town is close enough to Germany to share the same trolley bus system.

The name Nijmegen today is nearly as famous as that of Arnhem because of the airborne operations in 1944 when it was partially razed during the fighting. The British War Cemetery, where 1300 officers and men are buried, is near the Goffert Stadium. The Canadian cemetery is 6 miles (10 km) south at Groosbeek on a hill above the battlefield where they fought so tenaciously. There are 2500 Canadian graves. The third cemetery is a small one at Mook where 300 British lie at rest.

Hotel Nijmegen
This is an ETAP hotel, a chain comprising many hotels in Holland. Recently built, with 96 rooms, it is a first class establishment standing near the railway station in the centre of the town. It has an excellent bistro and a parking area alongside. The town square is picturesque and has a Weigh House dating from 1612. The famous Kerkboog is a vaulted passage with an elaborate gable built in 1606. In the nearby Laekenhall,

cloth merchants used to conduct their business. In the same square stands a statue of a certain notorious lady, Mariken van Nieumeghen, who, history relates, was seduced by Satan himself and lived with him for seven years until she was converted to Christianity.

Nijmegen is well known for its annual four day walk called *de Vierdaagse* (the Nijmegen Marches). About 20,000 people singly and in groups come from many places to take part in a hiking marathon. The British and other armies are usually well represented. Besides the participants many more thousands come to watch along the route, much as they do for the canal skating events. Various categories, depending on age and sex, have to cover so many miles a day. It is one of those occasions when happily there are no winners and no prizes. All the hikers must do to win a medal is complete the course, covering a selected distance each day, without dropping out.

Nijmegen has beautiful surroundings, unspoilt villages, wooded areas, parkland and a unique open air museum run by the Holy Land Foundation.

It is also worth noting that both there, and at Arnhem, it is possible to enjoy boat trips on their respective rivers, and this provides a pleasant change as well as a relaxing way of sightseeing.

Biblical Open Air Museum
Situated between Nijmegen and Groosbeek, the Biblical Open Air Museum consists of a number of tableaux laid out alongside a walk through 13 acres (5 ha) of woodland. Biblical scenes are portrayed, such as bedouin goat-hair tents where shepherds watch their flocks, which are live animals. Everything is life size and you feel the figures might turn round and talk to you. On a warm sunny day you can almost believe you are in Palestine or Jordan. There are squares where you can enter buildings and village streets with shuttered windows – even Pontius Pilate's palace. A stretch of water represents the Sea of Galilee. There are wine and olive presses, boats and fishing tackle, a synagogue and houses to walk through. These include two palatial ones belonging to Greek and Egyptian families. Monks will take you round or you can buy a booklet. The aim of the founder of this unusual place was to create a better understanding of the Bible by means of visual scenes for those who have not been to the Holy land.

Apeldoorn

Known as the largest Garden City in the Netherlands, Apeldoorn is 17 miles (27 km) north of Arnhem and attracts thousands of visitors annually. It is the shopping centre of the oldest and largest recreation area in Holland – the Veluwe. It has over 50 restaurants and nearly as many hotels, parks and camping sites. It has been said that every street is a park. Certainly most of them are tree-lined and often lead to a park. Its most beautiful castle (Het Loo) was, until recently, the summer residence of the Royal Family. When, after reigning for half a century, Queen Wilhelmina abdicated in 1948 it was to this castle that she retired, and she lived there until her death 14 years later. More recently it was the home of her grand-daughter, Princess Margriet, and Mr Pieter van Vollenhoven. Their youngest son, Floris, was christened in the chapel there in 1975.

Apeldoorn, despite its lavish villas and leisurely atmosphere, has also been well known for its paper industry. At the turn of the century many paper mills were turned into laundries, for the water of the Veluwe, like that of Manchester, is famous for its softness. It is said that Apeldoorn's laundries could take in the whole country's washing!

The town is spread out and develops into forests and villages such as Loenen, known for its waterfall – the highest in Holland – and the 700 acre (283 ha) Berg en Bos with sunken ornamental lakes, fountains and waterfalls. Thousands of roses bloom here and in the spring rhododendrons and other flowering shrubs stain the valleys with colour. The walks are fascinating and you can watch deer and wild boar in a large game reserve just off the Apeldoorn–Amersfoort road near the Aardhuis. In one of the royal forests there is an old well, dug on William III's orders to supply his foresters with water. It is said to be 200 ft (61 m) deep and is still in use.

Castle Het Loo

Het Loo, although small, is very beautiful, with a long façade. Visitors do not find it tiring walking through it, for every apartment, though charming, is compact.

In 1684 William III, Prince of Orange, and future King of England, bought this small fifteenth-century castle at Apeldoorn as a hunting lodge for the Royal Family. It took seven years of refurbishment before it met with his approval. It is a strange coincidence that the recent restoration also took seven years. It had remained one of the favourite castles of the Royal Orange-Nassau line for close on three centuries. The foundation stone was laid by Princess Mary Stuart of England in 1685. The gardens have always been carefully tended and it was said, during the reign of the Sun King of France, that they were even lovelier than those of Versailles. Today you can see them as they were originally designed in the seventeenth century, copied from paintings and drawings of that time. Walls have been rebuilt on their old foundations and inside them the parterres have been laid out again and planted with box hedging in decorative patterns. Shallow walls in front of the palace have terra cotta vases with plants which were cast from an original model that had survived. Facing the entrance staircase and surrounded by four parterres is a large fountain with sprays of water at different heights.

The first place you visit after wandering through the gardens is the Royal Stables, which were built between 1906 and 1910. Here there are coaches, carriages, vintage cars and sledges. The latter are elegantly designed, their curved runners resembling those you see in pictures of Czarist Russia, with a bowed front, low seating and drawn by plump horses. One of the paintings in the castle shows Queen Emma and Queen Wilhelmina in a silver sleigh, pulled by a pair of horses with royal purple plumes on their heads. Also on display here is a tiny car just big enough for a child to sit in. Its bonnet is outlined in mink! It was a gift from Prince Claus to his youngest son some years ago.

Corridors were not considered essential during the seventeenth century. The palace is divided into apartments leading into each other on either side of an axis. There is a central staircase and an upper hall. The

33 *Castle Het Loo at Apeldoorn*

chapel is small and simple with a pulpit opposite the entrance. A Bible belonging to William III is on a desk. When Queen Wilhelmina lay in state there in 1962 the Bible was placed on her coffin.

Two rooms in particular remind one of the indomitable Queen Wilhelmina. They are her sitting room and her study. Here, as well as her writing desk, is the Table of Resistance. This honours the Dutch Underground Movement of the Second World War and has a display of documents and publications which were illegal during the war.

The oldest apartments are those of King William III and Queen Mary. They are on the first floor and each has an antechamber, a bedroom (Queen Mary's has a bed which was sent to her from Kensington Palace in London), a dressing room and smaller rooms or closets. These closets are charming. Intimate and very small they are made from corners of larger rooms so that there are windows on two sides, a mantelpiece over an open fireplace takes up a third wall and a fourth has the door. A comfortable cushioned chair stands in front of the fireplace. The small sections of wall which can be seen are covered in red and green damask. Over the chimney piece is a portrait depicting the sacrifice of Abraham. On either side hang two silver sconces. On the hearth are silver mounted bellows, possibly English, as is a red lacquer cabinet supported by four Moors. Blue Delftware vases stand in the empty fireplace. With a blazing fire on a chilly winter evening it must have been snug and comfortable. Just outside stands an inviting book cabinet.

King William's closet is similar in many ways. His walls are in red and purple damask. A mirror is incorporated in the mantelpiece which has exquisite Delft vases. There are copper firedogs in front of his fireplace and French bronze sconces dating from 1700. Against one wall he has an ornate desk with over a dozen drawers topped with more Delftware.

The furniture at Het Loo is magnificent. In King William's bedroom you will see the only silver furniture in the Netherlands and whole suites are inlaid with mother of pearl and ivory. There are Chinese cabinets and exquisite Delftware. One longs to open the beautifully bound books in the library. The wall coverings of tooled leather, silk and damask are protected by perspex panelling to waist height, to avoid damage by visitors' clothing.

Some months before the departure of Princess Margriet from Castle Het Loo, the Royal Family decided to turn the place into a National Museum. It had acted as a temporary home for Dutch nationals who had to flee from Indonesia after the Second World War, and again for destitute victims of the Zeeland floods in 1953. Before it was opened to the public, Queen Juliana started a full-scale restoration scheme to return the castle to its seventeenth-century splendour. Queen Beatrix performed the opening ceremony on 20 June 1984.

Some interesting facts emerged during the restoration. The exterior of the palace had to be dismantled in places. Inside interesting discoveries were made. Seventeenth-century ceilings and wall paintings were revealed after the removal of layers of paint. In some parts the present interior was left untouched to show the influence of the different members of the House of Orange-Nassau. Many of the artefacts, paintings, tapestries and furniture belong to the Royal Collection.

Portraits and paintings are in profusion. Several cabinets in the East Wing act as a background for prints, medals, silverware, porcelain and ceramics. The first floor of the West Wing houses the collection of the Netherland's Orders of Knighthood. On the ground floor a 25 minute video programme with a commentary in Dutch, English, German or French explains the history and restoration details of the palace. Most parts of the building and gardens are open to the public. There are two restaurants and ample parking space for cars and coaches.

As a National Museum, Het Loo demonstrates the history of the House of Orange and its ties with the Netherlands since 1403. It is open throughout the year from 10 a.m. to 5 p.m. Guided tours are possible by appointment with Rijksmuseum Het Loo, Koninklijke Park 1, Apeldoorn, Netherlands; tel. 055 212244.

9
LIMBURG
AND
NORTH BRABANT

Limburg

In the most densely-populated area of Europe lies the province of Limburg in the delta of the Schelde, Maas and Rhine, close to Belgium, Luxembourg and Germany. In the tourist season coaches leave Maastricht, the capital, for trips through three countries. After breakfasting in Limburg you drink your morning coffee by a waterfall in the Belgian Ardennes (or in Brussels) and your aperitif in Luxembourg. You can sample German wine on the Rhine, Moselle or Ahr at your ease, or, if you do not have time to spare, before dinner you can easily be back in the province.

The extraordinary wedge-shaped province of Limburg was formed due to warring between small feudal states (during which the Duchy of Lower Lorraine was built up) in the second half of the eleventh century. In June 1288 the Duchies of Limburg and Brabant passed under the rule of a common sovereign. From 1794 to 1814 France included Limburg in the French Departments of Ourthe and Meuse Interieure. Belgium and Holland both laid claim to it in 1830 and Germany had political ties. Finally, at a conference of the great powers in London in 1866, it was agreed that Limburg should be an integral part of Dutch territory. It is 75 miles (120 km) long and 18¼ miles (29 km) wide and quite unlike other parts of Holland with a line of hills over 600 ft (182 m) high, called the Alps of Holland. At their base there are fertile valleys laced with rushing rivers. There are also coal mines which produce half the country's needs.

Venlo is the great salad bowl of Holland, a city of glass. Even as you enter it both sides of the road are lined with gleaming glass buildings stretching for miles in all directions. Tomatoes are grown here the year round and 80 per cent go to Germany. The Dutch farmers produce more per acre than seems possible in Europe. Every ray of the sun is utilized, and if you drive through the outskirts of Venlo on a sunny day the rows of glass houses seem to merge into glittering frozen lakes as far as you can see.

Although wars and sieges (especially the Second World War) have taken their toll on this old border town, a few major buildings have escaped serious damage. The church of St Martinus is thirteenth-century, and its tall tower has been repaired recently. Its interior is baroque with sculptures and paintings. The pulpit, upheld by an angel with outstretched arms, is very ornate and impressive. Opposite the church there is a Renaissance building of red brick with blue shutters. The house adjoining it is of the same era.

The Town Hall is also Renaissance in style, topped with two belfries. Inside, its council chamber is lined with Cordova leather. Sculptured lions guard the circular staircase before the façade where there are four statues of famous citizens of Venlo. The first is a painter, another a scientist, Jan van Clefe, after whom the local museum is named; the third figure is that of an astrologer, and the fourth of an eminent clockmaker called Venlo, after whom the town is named.

Perhaps because there are only a few factories in the town the atmosphere is very clear and it is preferred above others in Holland for astronomy. Gliding is also a great pastime.

Forestry and rose growing are other activities in this hilly area. The outskirts have lovely views over the Maas valley which is dotted with castles, several of which you can visit. One, close to the town, with a double moat and a splendid gateway, has been converted into a restaurant. In Limburg province there are over 100 castles and it also boasts Holland's only true mountain, the Dreilandenpunt near Vaals. It is some 1000 ft (300 m) high and overlooks Holland, Belgium and Germany. The symbol of Limburg is an unusual one, the nightingale.

The buildings of the Cooperative Venlo Auction Association, erected in 1965, are the largest in Europe. Unfortunately they are not open to the public except by invitation (which I was fortunate enough to get), and my host took me by car which is the only way you can go through the various halls if time is at a premium. Even so it is difficult to take in their grand scale. You see millions of boxes in the warehouses of fruit, vegetables and flowers awaiting shipment. More than 100 million guilders worth of produce is sold every year and all of it is grown in the north of Limburg. Venlo holds a flower exhibition each year.

I found that watching flowers being auctioned was rather like a game of roulette. Large dials, hung on one wall of the auction rooms, were controlled by the auctioneers. The rest of the hall facing these walls was lined with rows of desks in raised tiers. Each desk is equipped with a telephone. Gigantic trolleys loaded with flowers – all the same colour and stem length – are pushed into a space before the desks by men clad in grey coats. One of them holds a sample bunch of flowers aloft and the bidding begins, each one being indicated to everyone by the dials. As soon as one trolley load is sold, in comes the next. At Christmas time tons of mistletoe and holly are sold in the same way. The cooling rooms are far too cold to visit for long, and there are restaurants for the buyers and scores of offices for the employees.

Carnival time in Limburg takes place during the three days preceding Ash Wednesday. In Venlo young couples dress up in old fashioned clothes with wing collars, lace bonnets and jabots and ride in carriages to be 'married' by the burgomaster. The men have artificial side whiskers and wear black hats like bowlers; the brides carry green bunches of kale tied up with bright ribbons. The streets are full of merrymakers who cheer the carriages on to the Town Hall where more people wait to toast the couples' happiness.

Thorn

Not far from Venlo is the border town of Thorn. It was once an independent kingdom with its own coinage. Its Gothic Abbey, around which small white houses and the Town Hall are built, was founded towards the end of the tenth century by Ansfrey, a Count of Maas, and later the Bishop of Utrecht and his wife Hereswift took it over. In the late Middle Ages the abbey and its lands were administered by an abbess and her canonesses, all from noble families, and the abbey became rich. When the French invaded in 1797 the treasure was confiscated, but happily the church itself was undamaged.

The abbey is a most unusual place to visit. The interior is white, with slender pillars crowned by acanthus leaf carving. A semicircular staircase of white wrought-iron faces the choir and above the altar there is a sculpture of the birth of Christ. The windows are of plain glass so that the light shines through emphasizing the white. Outside the spires are striped with white lines, and Thorn, known as the White Town, has a quiet charm not often found today. Lines of houses, with window boxes full of brightly coloured flowers, line cobbled streets. All are white and cluster about the white abbey. In the tiny square before the church stands the Town Hall, in front of which a large black eagle is worked into the cobbles. It was built in 1960, but in the old style. When a house needs repairing it is done with old bricks or excellent imitations. I watched workmen remake a wall with bricks that matched and had been taken from another wall no longer needed.

There are two hotels in Thorn: La Ville Blanche fronted by a box hedge and the Hotel Crasborn. You enter the Crasborn through a tiled hallway. In summer you can eat in the garden; otherwise there is an indoor restaurant. Oil lamps hang from the ceiling and there is a Victorian bar at the far end. If you stop there for tea you must order the local shortbread which is delicious and a speciality of the town.

Asselt

Not far from Thorn is the village of Asselt which has a charming Romanesque church encircled with roses known as the Church of the Roses. It dates from the eleventh century and is one of the oldest churches in Holland. Clusters of white roses bloom in front of it and on the right side pink ones flourish. The church itself is tiny with a double-vaulted ceiling. Kneeling chairs covered in worn yellow velvet line the pews. A children's chapel built in 1917 is to the right of the altar and the sacristy is to the left, where there are two small stained-glass windows, one depicting the Flight into Egypt. These were made by Nicholas in 1925. Above the altar itself light filters through a rose window.

In Roman times the church was a building where people had to pay dues to cross over the river. It was rebuilt as a compact Norman castle before being turned into a church. The eleventh-century font has a brass cover with a handle in the form of a figure of Christ on the Cross. If the verger is present he will take you to the little museum across the road. It is full of all kinds of bric-a-brac from antlers and suits of armour to china and pewter.

A mile or so away from the Church of the Roses a splendid castle, Hillenraad, is still privately owned, but the grounds can be seen by arrangement.

Maastricht

Maastricht is Holland's oldest city. Although the river Maas separates Belgium and Holland, Maastricht lies on both sides of it, bulging out on the western bank like a great sack. Even in prehistoric days there was a settlement on this site and during the Middle Ages Maastricht was well known for its ecclesiastical leanings and today is mainly a Roman Catholic city.

St Servatius Bridge and Church were named after the city's first bishop and patron saint, an Armenian missionary, who had been Bishop of Tongres and moved his See to Maastricht. He lived there until his death in AD 384 and for the next three centuries Maastricht was the See of some 20 bishops. One of the town landmarks, a high pillar with a bronze image of the Virgin Mary, is flanked by statues of four of them. Of these, Lambertus was the only one to be born in the city. This was in the eighth century and he was succeeded by Hubertus who moved the seat of the bishopric to Liège. This led to an odd situation. The bishops continued to rule Maastricht from Liège but eventually had to share their sway with the Dukes of Brabant. So began the strange binary government of Maastricht.

People soon took advantage of this situation and played one Lord off against the other. The city fathers coined the phrase 'One Lord, no Lord, two Lords, one Lord'. Another point was that citizens could change their nationality once during their lifetimes, becoming either Dutch or Belgian. The Town Hall could be entered by two staircases so that one Lord did not have to precede the other.

The Town Hall was built in the eleventh century and is in the centre of the town square, which is unique. It is said to have been a zone of safety in the old days when wars and sieges were rife. If citizens fled there they were free, even if the rest of the town fell. It is often thought that this is the reason why an enormous square survives in such a small city as Maastricht, but this is not so. Originally is was a tiny independent state under the Provost of the Chapter of St Servatius and was at that time protected by a high fortified wall. It is one of the most fascinating squares in Holland.

The patrician houses opposite the Town Hall have an attractive mixture of façades – Renaissance, baroque and rococo. In the Town Hall itself (which was built by the same architect who designed the Dam in Amsterdam, Pieter Post) the ceilings are richly painted. The Liège room and other chambers are hung with tapestries and paintings. The Prince's room has large Flemish tapestries completely covering its walls, depicting biblical scenes such as Moses crossing the Red Sea.

The two statues in the square seem to listen as the carillon chimes from the Town Hall tower. One is of a pregnant-looking country housewife who is bringing vegetables to sell. She wears a cloak and cap. An apron falls over her ample skirt and, as she listens, an amused smile is on her lips. Quite different is the dignified figure of Minckelers, across the square, a scholar of Maastricht who discovered that gas could be made from coal. The apparatus which he made to do this stands behind him. Two weekly markets are held in the square, a small one on Wednesdays and a large one on Fridays.

Amongst the many cafés and restaurants which line the square you can easily spot the earlier Town Hall with its dignified Gothic façade. It was here that William the Silent was outlawed in the name of the King of Spain during the Eighty Years War.

To the west side of the nearby Vrijthof square soars the St Servatius Cathedral, parts of which, including the crypt, are sixth-century. The porch is outstanding in that it is one of the earliest examples of Gothic sculpture in Europe. A gilt reliquary in the crypt is said to contain bones of St Servatius. Romanesque in style, it is known as the 'Emergency Chest' because during times of strife it was often carried through the streets to comfort the populace.

The cathedral was considerably enlarged in the fourteenth and fifteenth centuries. The beautiful entrances are decorated with statuettes.

The largest clock in the Netherlands hangs in the middle tower in the west wall; called 'Grameer' (Grandmother) it weighs 15,400 lb (7000 kg). At the back of the cathedral stands a statue of Charlemagne. The treasury houses a collection of religious objects and both cathedral and treasury can be visited, but not during services.

34 *Maastricht*

St Janskerk, the Protestant church to one side of St Servatius, was formerly the cathedral's baptistry. It is a fine Gothic building with a 230 ft (70 m) tower which is square to three-quarters of its height and then becomes octagonal before reaching the spire.

The narrow streets in the area are well worth a stroll. Restoration has been going here for the last ten years and the results are rewarding. Old signs have been reworked, marble swags and statuary repaired on house fronts, ancient inns and shops reopened. The cobbled streets have runnels down the centre to drain off excessive rain. Many of the signs are in French and the inns have peculiar names – the Three Crowned Herrings, Reynard the Fox, The Angel, the Golden Swan, the Unicorn, the Ostrich, Golden Brandy Cauldron.

The many-arched stone bridge of St Servatius replaced a wooden one as long ago as 1280 and was rebuilt in 1683. Less impressive is the second bridge, the Wilhelmina, which spans the river and was erected in 1934.

Near St Servatius Bridge stands a jester-like statue which typifies the spirit of Maastricht. The people speak a special dialect, perhaps because they are so close to other countries. They are good linguists and French, German and English come easily to them. Wines are excellent and reasonable in price, many coming from France. The local gin is called *els* and the town's apple pies and gingerbread are famous.

The three-and-a-half days before Lent are carnival time. Prince Carnival, elected by a committee, is crowned in the Town Hall and opens the ceremonies with an amusing speech poking fun at the Establishment. He wears a medieval costume of doublet and hose, with a white silk jester's hat. He is accompanied to the hall by the Stovepipers band who look very Scots in their kilts, white spats and jabots, and the Farmers band who wear blue smocks and flat hats.

The Mayor presents the Prince with the keys of the city for his brief reign, a large rustic doll called the Vegetable Woman or *Moosweef* is hoisted above the square and the festivities begin. Processions march round the town clad in funny clothes, false noses and cardboard hats and it is a time of dancing, feasting and drinking. Everyone joins in the fun.

One of the things to do in Maastricht is take a walk along what remains of the old city walls. Much skill and energy went into the building of two walls of fortification to discourage raids and sieges which were common in the Middle Ages. The ramparts were dismantled some time after 1871. From the wall you can gaze across the road towards parkland which fringes the river. It is dotted with various kinds of trees through which you can see the blue water and, beyond the river, the other section of Maastricht known as Wijk. When you reach the Helpoort (the Gateway to Hell) you will see a bulwark behind it called the Five Heads, where at one time five heads were displayed of men beheaded because they had crossed swords with the local Duke. It is said that d'Artagnan of *The Three Musketeers* fame was also killed here.

Walking along the walls you come to a short flight of steps leading up from the Pest House where victims of the Plague were cared for long ago (it was later turned into a water mill). Nearby is a picturesque complex of old buildings of grey stone, and a turreted water gate. Back at ground level you return to everyday life with a pedestrian precinct and shopping mall. Also, not far away, is St Amorsplein, a little square where this patron saint of lovers looks out benevolently from his high pillar. People sit at small tables below sipping drinks or having tea while they make up their minds where to go next.

Mount St Peter

Two miles south of the city is the strange tunnelled hill of St Peter's Mount, a very curious place. It has interested visitors for centuries and amongst the hundreds of signatures inscribed on the subterranean walls are those of Napoleon, the Duke of Alba, Sir Walter Scott, Voltaire and the Prince of Orange. In one passage a sombre note is added by the words 'Four monks, gone astray in this cavern, found death in 1640'.

The Mount covers one of the most unusual fortresses in Europe. For centuries limestone blocks were excavated from the site to build churches, fortifications and Maastricht itself. Gradually a labyrinth of underground galleries came into being which proved invaluable for military purposes.

The French under Louis XIV turned it into a fortress and later military engineers built a winding staircase to connect more galleries. In 1794 the French attacked again and fighting actually took place down in the tunnels. During the ensuing siege they tried to blow the place sky high, but only succeeded in blocking up many of the galleries. When Maastricht fell the French studied the fortress once more and one of the scientists wrote a book about it which was later published in Paris. In war time the passages proved both a blessing and a curse. As a place of refuge they were safe, but many fugitives got lost, starved and died, though some were found and led to safety. During the Spanish wars they were used to hide peasants and farm animals.

In the last war, Allied servicemen were hidden by the Dutch or led through thc tunnels into Belgium. Local guides were essential and the Germans dared not enter. Many of the chambers were used as safety vaults for national treasures, the most famous of which was Rembrandt's *Night Watch*. Towards the end of the war, in case of an emergency, the people of Maastricht made Mount St Peter virtually an underground town for some thousands of people. Facilities included electricity, dormitories, a chapel, library, bakery and hospital.

Guides can show you much of interest today. At one time this quarried mountain was beneath the sea, as can be seen by the fossils, the most important one being a giant turtle 3 ft (1 m) long. Sharks' teeth, amongst other prehistoric objects, are embedded in the limestone. Some galleries are used for mushroom and chicory growing, the former looking like made beds with smooth dark counterpanes embroidered with white flowers.

The temperature is constant in the galleries and from October to April bats hibernate in some of them. As they have no body 'thermostat' it is necessary for them to avoid the open air during their long sleep. Since 1937 research has been done on the bats and an interesting point is that most of them return to the same place year after year. They are ringed with small discs noting type, sex, date and place of ringing. After many years it is now known that Mount St Peter is second only to the Carlsbad Cavern in New Mexico as a hibernation refuge for bats.

Valkenburg

You will find other underground catacombs at Valkenburg, some 8 miles (13 km) east of Maastricht on the way to Heerlen. Valkenburg is referred to as the Swiss part of Holland and also the Highlands of the Netherlands. Certainly the hill tops rise about 1000 ft (300 m) and this pretty town entices visitors not only from abroad but also from the rest of Holland. In the summer months the population doubles.

Two branches of the River Geul divide the town and as well as several hotels there are some good restaurants. Special mention must be made of the Prinses Juliana, which has earned two stars in the *Guide Michelin* and is one of the best eating places in the country. Prices are not outrageous and the menu includes scampi flambee, smoked Dutch salmon and saddle of lamb cooked with herbs from their own garden. From mid-October there is a choice of excellent game. Wine cellars run beneath the garden terraces and the wine list, as in several places in Limburg, is comprehensive. International taste is catered for, even Christmas pudding for the British. The hotel is small with some 30 rooms and is featured in two other French guides: *Guide Relais et Chateaux* and *Traditions et Qualité*.

Valkenburg's well-known casino is in the centre of town in the Odapark. You enter it across a wooden bridge over the River Geul. The gaming room has 13 roulette and five black jack tables and a spacious bar. A short flight of steps leads you into the restaurant – Le Jardin. Everything here is art deco with reproductions of the chairs from the Fledermaus Cabaret in Vienna, a reminder of the atmosphere of its heyday. There is a smaller, more intimate room with two roulette tables and its own little bar. A separate television room enables guests to watch programmes from Holland, Belgium and Germany.

There are four main casinos in Holland, at Scheveningen, Rotterdam, Valkenburg and the fourth, not so far mentioned, at Zandvoort, half an hour's drive from Amsterdam. It was the first of the four to be opened in 1976.

Castles dot Valkenburg and the surrounding districts. Even the provincial tourist office is appropriately placed in the Castle Den Helder. On high crags overlooking the town there are the remains of a castle that dominated the area for centuries. Inside its walls the fate of the lands between the Rhine and the Schelde were decided. It was repeatedly destroyed and rebuilt, but disaster really struck in 1672 when it was blown up. Even so the remains still stand to dominate the skyline. Part of the Knight's Hall is intact and there are still secret passages to casemates and grottos below ground.

Municipal grottos

These consist of extensive underground corridors not formed by nature, but hewn out of the soft marlstone by man. The Romans once quarried material here to build their villas and defence works. There is an underground lake and some natural caves which have always proved useful in time of war, especially the Second World War, when they acted as shelters like those in Maastricht. Today you can go through them on a little sightseeing train. You will see mural paintings, sculptures, fossils and layers of prehistoric shells. Even more interesting perhaps are the Roman catacombs. These are replicas of 14 of the best known catacombs of Rome. They were excavated in 1909 and took four years to complete. Candlelight tours are most realistic and it seems strange that you can admire part of early Christian Rome not in Italy but in Holland.

You can also visit an artificial coal mine. The marlstone is easily cut and drilled so everything has been made as realistic as possible. All the sounds of a working mine are reproduced by loudspeakers. The drilling of holes, insertion of explosive charges and blasting are all demonstrated by working miners as they enlarge the mine. You can see the compressed air lines, miners' lanterns, telephone system and all the other impedimenta of a modern coal mine.

Valkenburg was first visited by tourists in the nineteenth century and over the years has added to its many attractions. There is an open air theatre, a zoo, an aquarium, Klant's wild animal training school, night clubs, swimming pools and well-marked walking trails. For a small sum children may paint their own designs on pottery vases and have them glazed and fired within 24 hours.

Tegelem

One Limburg town, Tegelem, is reminiscent of Oberammergau. It is about 2 miles (3 km) south of Venlo, and a Passion Play is performed there every five years by the local people. They have made an open air theatre where rehearsals take two years and over 500 players perform. The original play was written by a local priest and is more or less the same each time. It depicts Christ as a modern social reformer.

Margraten Military Cemetery

Three miles (5 km) south of Valkenburg on the main Maastricht/Aachen highway you come to the Margraten Military Cemetery, which reminds one of Arnhem. It is where the American dead who fell in Holland have been buried (except for those bodies which have since been removed to their home cemeteries in America). Nearly 18,000 soldiers are buried here. Row after row of white crosses line the green grass. Beside the simple chapel there is a statue of a woman which is reflected in a rectangular pool. Her figure is draped and birds wing over her right shoulder. As in Arnhem, local families have adopted graves and place flowers and wreaths on them on special remembrance occasions.

Gulpen

Before visiting Neubourg Castle, if time allows, you should stop at the trout hatcheries. Like the castle they are in Gulpen and are open from May to October. Until the last war Limburg's rivers produced 500,000 salmon a year and most of these went to nearby Belgium. Later, increased industry alongside the rivers polluted many of the streams, and hatcheries were the only answer to the problem. These have flourished so that they yield 7000 to 150,000 trout a year. Hatcheries can salvage 95 per cent of the eggs whereas natural circumstances only yield about 5 per cent, the rest being eaten, swept away or lost through other hazards.

Castle Neubourg Hotel

The Castle Neubourg has been owned by the Ansembourg family since its completion. When the Count died the Countess found the castle too large and, keeping some rooms for herself, rented the rest as an hotel. You drive through an archway into a courtyard to the front entrance. Inside the furnishings are lavish. Persian carpets cover the floors and crystal chandeliers hang from high ceilings. The main lounge is decorated in dark green and gold with comfortable chairs and sofas. The dining room, with white walls and a partially gilded ceiling, has a lobster tank in one corner, but if you do not feel like tackling one, there is excellent smoked eel and a large choice of other fresh fish beside the usual grills. The wine list is extensive.

You go up to the bedrooms by a gracious shallow staircase and come face to face with a floor to ceiling mirror at a bend. You get an Alice-through-the-looking-glass feeling when you suddenly realize that you must not walk into the reflection, but turn sharp right. The bedrooms have canopied beds and large windows through which you can see the castle grounds with their formal gardens.

Dreilandenpunt

Continuing along the road from Gulpen to Vaals, where there are many restaurants, cafés and hotels, you come to a unique area where three countries meet at Dreilandenpunt. It is Holland's highest point, 1021 ft (311 m), and overlooks Holland, Belgium and Germany. The only access to the hill is from the Dutch side, and hikers with national identity cards or passports are allowed to use trails going through the three countries without any barriers. However, human nature being what it is, a little smuggling does go on. For instance, cigarettes are cheaper in Belgium than in the other two countries. Customs men do check people now and then. Five packets of cigarettes are allowed in duty free. The forest walks are marked with signs at the base of tree trunks in blue, yellow and red indicating the distances. The woodlands here are glorious and a plinth marks the exact spot where the three countries meet.

The Belgian coast

If you cross from England to Holland with your car by ferry and arrive at Zeebrugge this port has an interesting museum covering the history of the port in the two World Wars. Heist is the first place you come to, with a small fishing port. Duinbergen is a small garden city. At Albertstrand you will find a casino which also has a cinema and theatre. During the season the theatre has international artists in its programme to add to the gambling and night club facilities. Inland behind it is the luxurious La Reserve Hotel under the same management as the casino. Guests enjoy free entry to both casino and night club. Crimson and blue suites are fitted with wall safes – presumably for winnings – and there is a private lake for swimming and boating. Knokke is the business hub of the Belgian coast with delightful shops and numerous hotels.

Zoute, nearest to the Dutch border, has charming villas, woods and gardens and is a residential area. The Rustlaan is the main shopping street. The former summer residence of King Leopold III is in the Zwin, a 300 acre (120 ha) nature reserve lying partly in Belgium and partly in Holland. It is often flooded and contains unique bird and plant life.

North Brabant

North Brabant, the largest province in Holland, is the central southern area of the country. In the east, near the German border, you will find Overloon with its Netherlands National War and Resistance Museum. It is an open air museum covering some 40 acres (16 ha) of parkland. It was the scene of one of the most violent tank battles of the last war, which took place in the autumn of 1944. The village was razed and more than 300 wrecked tanks were left behind. Some of these can still be seen together with aircraft, guns and other military equipment. Smaller weapons can be found in an armoury which has an Allied and German section. A nearby building contains thousands of documents and pictures relating to the last war and there is a separate department exclusively devoted to concentration camps and prisons. The museum is closed in December, January and February.

Eindhoven

The most industrial town in North Brabant is Eindhoven, headquarters of the enormous Philips combine, known as the City of Light. It is hard to believe that this bustling metropolis had barely 5000 inhabitants in 1900, although it received its charter more than seven centuries ago. In 1891 Dr A. F. Philips built an electric light bulb factory and gave it his name. Today it is the largest electronics company outside America and now employs thousands of people not only in Eindhoven but in many other countries.

When it celebrated its seventy-fifth anniversary it built the 98 ft (30 m) high Evoluon in the city. It has been likened to a gigantic flying saucer or a mighty mushroom. The great circular moon-shaped creation seemingly floats in the air (at night it is brilliantly lit from below) but it is held aloft by a series of V-shaped pillars. The Evoluon symbolizes what science can do for man in the evolution of technology. It is not the kind of exhibition where you just look at things passively. There certainly is a lot to see but there is also much to do. You can operate a number of models and machines yourself. You can discover what constitutes a sodium atom, how fast your reactions are and how a video telephone works. There is a test for colour blindness, instant playback recording and explanations are available in English. You will find the Evoluon on the north-west edge of the city at the junction of the ring road with the road to Tilburg.

Eindhoven is also known for its many and excellent shops, especially in its pedestrian precinct where there are over 200. It is a centre for conventions, among the larger meeting places being the Institute of Technology and the Philips Ontspanningscentrum. There are places of interest in the town centre. Close to one another are the modern Gothic style Town Hall, a church by Cuijpers – St Catherina – and the Museum Kempenland containing local archaeological finds. The Van Abbemuseum, with a permanent collection and changing exhibitions, is concerned mainly with the visual arts of the present century.

Tilburg

This used to be an important textile town of which the Netherlands Textile Museum is a reminder. It has a modern theatre with adjoining restaurant. The Town Hall is elegant – small wonder as it was once the palace of William II. Near the town is the well-known Beekse Bergen safari park, zoo and recreation area, and 7 miles (11 km) north is a Disney-like park called De Efteling covering 700 acres (280 ha). It brings fairy tales to life even to the enchanted tower of the sleeping beauty. Playgrounds are not forgotten – there is boating and swimming, a merry-go-round, pony rides and a puppet theatre.

35   *The famous Dutch wooden clogs*

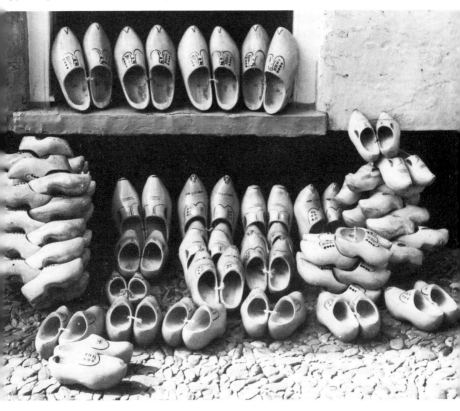

Best

Seven miles (11 km) north-west of Eindhoven is the town of Best, renowned for its clog making since early times. The clog museum, De Platijn, is delightful. Here you can see how clogs are made by hand from blocks of willow or poplar, and there are scenes from a cobbler's house of a century ago when his workshop was part of his home. Dutch wooden shoes have always been famous and few visitors can resist buying them, whether they be minute Delft blue china ones for decoration or large wooden ones to use as unusual plant pots when they get home. Then there are those for everyday use, some of which have soles of hardwood, leather uppers but no back part. At Best they make literally thousands of them so there is plenty of choice, but of course you can buy them almost anywhere in Holland as they are so popular. They must be one of the oldest types of footwear known to man and it is a curious fact that they were the model used by the American astronauts for their moonwalking footwear.

Hertogenbosch

Called Den Bosch by locals this fascinating town is the capital of North Brabant, lying 18 miles (30 km) north-west of Eindhoven. The name means the Dukes Woods and it was founded by Duke Henry of Brabant in the twelfth century. In 1985 the city celebrated its eight-hundredth anniversary. It grew up around its market place which boasts a baroque Town Hall, its council chamber hung with paintings by famous Dutch artists including Theodoor Thulden, one of Rubens' talented pupils. When the Town Hall clock strikes the hour there is the melodious sound of a carillon of 38 bells. This accompanies a battle display by miniature knights in armour on the façade.

The square's famous statue is of Hieronymus Bosch, the painter, born here in 1450. An exhibition of his work was held in the town in 1967 and drew 270,000 visitors. His strange surrealist paintings are now held in great regard. Holland possesses only three of his works, the remainder being in galleries all round the world.

Saint Jan's Cathedral

This elegant edifice is one of the most beautiful of its kind in Europe. Pure Gothic, it is in the form of a Latin cross with delicate flying buttresses. Its nave is supported by 150 slender columns and there are a number of important things to see: the highly decorated choir stalls, a Renaissance chair, a copper baptismal font (1492), fine statuary and two paintings by Bosch – the *Virgin with Child* and *St Jan* (John). The cathedral was constructed between 1330 and 1530 on the foundations of a previous church which burned down in 1240. It suffered heavy damage

1 many wars and was again restored in 1860 and 1955.

Of particular interest are the grotesque creatures scampering over the flying buttresses reminiscent of those in Hieronymus Bosch's paintings, and there is a possibility that he may have been responsible for their design. If you are sitting in an outdoor café near the cathedral and have binoculars, take a good look at the little people on the walls. A local tale has it that each time you drink a pint of beer they change their positions!

North Brabant Museum

This museum contains items relating to the arts, history and crafts of the province. There are collections of coins, weapons, prints, manuscripts, pewter, silver and copper. Special exhibitions are arranged throughout the year.

Breda

Breda is in the centre of Brabant on the Amsterdam–Paris road a few miles from the Belgian frontier. It takes about 45 minutes to drive to Rotterdam and to the south you can reach Antwerp in the same time. The city is a mixture of old world charm and industrial tumult. The vast Hero factory is noted for its canned fruit, vegetables and soft drinks.

Breda's defences were first laid out in 1534 and it is still a garrison town. Its castle is the present Royal Military Academy and has a background of historical events, the most stirring being in the 'Wooden Horse' tradition. When the Spanish captured it in 1590 a group of Dutch soldiers were smuggled aboard a barge and hidden beneath a load of peat. The innocent boatman got permission to take his barge through the watergate into the castle and, when he had moored, the Dutch guerrillas stormed ashore and not only recaptured the castle but regained the whole town.

King Charles II of England spent part of his exile after the Cromwell débâcle in Breda Castle. Breda was also the place where the Dutch and the English signed the peace treaty which made New Amsterdam (New York) English. There are other castles in this charming town and 16,000 acres (6500 ha) of woodland. For the visitor there are several hotels, restaurants and two large motels in the outskirts.

The Reformed church contains fine monuments to the early Counts of Nassau-Dillenburg including Duke Engelbrecht II, who founded the present Royal House of Orange-Nassau.

Of the other North Brabant towns, mention must be made of Roosendaal which has a small replica of St Peter's Church in Rome. Willemstad (named after William the Silent) on the Schelde estuary, has an attractive fishing harbour and an old fortress shaped like a seven-pointed star.

Zundert is famed not only as the birthplace of Vincent van Gogh but also because of its annual flower parade on the first Sunday of September which rivals that of Nice. Floats are festooned with as many as 100,000 blooms and it is one of the most lavish of the Dutch flower pageants

GRONINGEN
AND
FRIESLAND

The province of Groningen

Some time ago my first visit to Groningen, the most northerly province of Holland, provided an uncommon experience. We drove out of the capital (which has the same name) to the east, along route E35, and soon came to a large electricity generating plant with chimneys 400 ft (120 m) high. The flat countryside here is laced with canals and these were steaming. White clouds of vapour rose into the air and when my host, Jan Kappenburg, whose knowledge of his province is encyclopaedic, saw my incredulity he laughed: 'We are used to this sight. When the hot water from the plant runs into the cold water of the canals it causes steam to rise.' It was odd driving along a straight level road and suddenly having everything blotted out as if by a Scotch mist. Once or twice I had the illusion of being in cloud in the Alps until the vapour dispersed and again the road stretched ahead. 'If the wind is in a certain direction it is as bad as driving through fog,' continued Jan, 'but luckily this does not often happen.'

No sooner had we left our steaming canals behind than ships appeared on the horizon, as if one rounded a bend in the desert in Egypt and saw shipping in the Suez Canal. Ship building was in progress high on the canal bank. Jan pointed out one coaster which had been completed and was ready for launching. The ships are built on blocks and, when they are completed, these are knocked away and the ship is launched sideways into the canal. The big splash often floods the opposite bank and even the roadway, which is closed when a launching takes place. It is typical of Groningen Province and an impressive sight which attracts spectators.

We passed a number of wood processing factories, mostly Swedish. Then, at Slochteren, we came upon endless lines of natural gas drillings with thin tall pipes dispersing waste gases into the sky in quivering orange flames. Almost overnight this town became famous because of the treasure beneath its soil – the largest known deposit of natural gas in the world. It is supplied to Germany, Belgium and France as well as Holland.

Gradually we left the gas installation and came to Helligerlee, a small town 21 miles (34 km) east of Groningen and close to Winschoten. It claims two distinctions, that of being the main producer of cardboard in Europe and of having a world-famous bell foundry which produces complete carillons or bells of any size.

Our morning coffee break was Winschoten, the municipal centre of East Groningen. It is a natural stopping place along the Green Coast Road, the international tourist route between Scandinavia and the west of Holland. It is about 23 miles (37 km) from the city of Groningen and close to the German border. Three of its old windmills are prettily illuminated at night and it has several hotels and a well-equipped camping site where we had our coffee in the restaurant. The proprietor told me that the camping season began about the middle of May and continued until late summer. We bade goodbye and drove on to the border along a double highway to see the tourist office at the frontier.

Ter Apel

Later we went to Ter Apel, 36 miles (58 km) south-east of Groningen, to visit the medieval monastery. It is deep in a splendid beech wood and for some unknown reason is the only remaining one out of 30 that once graced the province. It is well worth seeing and was originally founded as a Premonstratensian (a canonical order founded in 1119) monastery in the thirteenth century. It was rebuilt in 1464 by the Crutched Friars (Domus novae Lucis) and has been used by the Dutch Reformed Church since 1604. Its smooth exterior walls are pierced by long, arched windows with tracery at their tops. The roofing is fluted and surmounted by an open circular belfry.

The interior is a lofty noble shell with a ceiling of Gothic vaulting soaring up from mid-wall ribs. One portion has a chapel with sculptured pews. When the choir seats are tipped up there are carved faces and other motifs underneath. A baptismal font stands in one of the cloisters and a few paintings of late bishops adorn one wall.

By the time we left the monastery dusk was falling and we returned to Groningen by a different route, the first 22 miles (35 km) of which ran alongside a straight wide canal on the way to Assen. Houses lined the far side of the canal and, as it grew dark and the lights came on, the living rooms were reflected in the still water. It is odd that the Dutch, so formal in many ways and respectful of their neighbour's privacy, never seem to draw their curtains at night. I could see children doing their homework, mothers preparing meals or sewing, fathers watching the news on television and dogs or cats on hearth rugs by the fireside. To see such scenes, reflected upside down, gave an Alice-in-Wonderland atmosphere. I mentioned this to Jan, who said 'It is sometimes said in

Groningen that if you do not have time to finish seeing a television murder mystery because you have to go out somewhere, you can easily discover who murdered whom, even if you turn your set off. Leave your car at home and go by bus. You can then watch other people's television sets through their uncurtained windows as you are driven along!'

Soon we were driving past Town Canal, a large complex of shops with rows of houses, a theatre and cinemas stretching back over a mile (2 km). Before the days of the car, when people wished to visit someone several miles away, it was as usual to go in a boat drawn along the canals by a horse as it was to go by carriage. After passing the small townships of Gieten and Rolde we soon reached Assen where we joined the double highway leading into Groningen.

The city of Groningen

Groningen is the most important town in the north of Holland, with wide streets, canals and sixteenth- and seventeenth-century houses whose eaves have a cramped picturesqueness. Its well-known university, founded in 1614, is in classical style. Among the university buildings, which are spread throughout the city, is an observatory and a library where the *pièce de résistance* is a copy of Erasmus' *New Testament* with marginal annotations by Luther. The University Hospital, continually expanding, is the medical centre for this part of the country. The students add a note of gaiety to the town, during term time, with their colourful caps, each denoting a different faculty: green for economics, white for law, red for medicine, blue for theology, pink for chemistry and yellow for mathematics.

The oldest part of the city is still surrounded by a former moat, and the residential section is dotted with pleasant gardens. In the centre of the town the Grote Markt is one of the largest market squares in the Netherlands and joining it is another square, the Vismarkt. The cluster of important buildings in the square is dominated by the 315 ft (96 m) Martini Tower, part of St Martin's church which has watched over Groningen for centuries. Even in 1945 when most of the city centre was razed during the German retreat, the Martini Tower remained unscathed. Its five storied spire looks as though it had sprung up like a jack-in-a-box, each section smaller than the one below and the fifth one topped by an open belfry. It is particularly impressive seen from across Shipcanal – *Schuitendiep* – one of the town's old moats. It is possible to climb the tower and see the carillon keyboard and automatic chiming mechanism, which plays every 15 minutes. A most rewarding part of the climb is the superb view over the city from the top. Look upwards and you will find that the weather vane has a little horse facing into the wind instead of the usual cockerel.

The church itself is Romanesque-Gothic. Stained-glass windows in the choir gallery, with the coats-of-arms of the Captain of the Civic Guard, were designed in 1770. The organ dates from 1480 and was built by a well-known musician and scholar, Rudolph Agricolo, who was born near Groningen in 1443. In recent times it has been restored and enlarged.

The Prinsenhof, sometimes referred to as the House with the Three Gates, close by St Martin's church, was the fifteenth-century priory of the Brotherhood of the Common Life. Nowadays it houses the regional broadcasting system and exhibitions are held there. From 15 March to 15 October its seventeenth-century garden is open from 9 a.m. until half an hour after sunset. Its enchanting 1738 sundial has a Latin proverb inscribed on it – 'The past is nothing, the future uncertain, the present unsteady. Do not lose your own time.' There are tree-sheltered walks, a herb garden, and roses bloom throughout the season in this quiet retreat.

Other buildings in the Grote Markt include the Goudkantoor (Gold Office) and, next to this, the neo-classical Town Hall connected by a glass enclosed bridgewalk to the New Town Hall. Not far away at 3 Naber Passage is the Tourist Information Office.

The seventeenth-century Gold Office, a Renaissance building, was the former Tax Office. Written across its façade is the Latin inscription 'Give to the Emperor his due'. Between its rectangular windows, which have bell-shaped scroll work above them, are attractive fleur de lys decorations. The roof is embellished with further scroll work. At night, when the buildings in the square are illuminated, it is particularly beautiful.

The canals, which encircle the town rather as they do in Amsterdam, are lined with golden lights in scallop design which reflect in the water. The humpbacked bridges are also edged in the same way and you can look beneath them and seemingly the golden dots reach to infinity along the black satiny water. Each year at Christmas time, behind an illuminated fountain in the Grote Markt, a tall green pine from Norway is set up, its lights swinging in the breeze.

A tower of the A-Church dominates the Vismarkt as the Martini tower does the Grote Markt. This church was founded in 1253 and rebuilt in the fifteenth century in Gothic style with its Renaissance tower, the top of which is called the Lantern. Chestnut trees edge the square and a section of it is used for a colourful flower market. When the chestnuts bloom Groningen holds its ten-day fair in the centre, adding a further kaleidoscope of colour.

The rivers of the province meet at Groningen, coming from the Drentse plateau, and the capital is an important shipping town for both inland and sea traffic. The river Drentse A is different in that one bank is much lower than the other, and they are known as the Highside of the A –

where lovely old patrician houses and warehouses are reflected in the water – and the Lowside of the A. Barges land their cargoes when the tide is out on the Lowside and vice versa.

Groningen is horse breeding country and its horses are famous. The British Royal Family have imported them for years and some of the Royal carriages are drawn by them. One of the sights in the capital is pairs of trotting horses drawing black and gold coaches. The coachmen wear silk hats. They can be hired and are used for all sorts of occasions. White carriages are traditional for weddings. When a married couple set off for their honeymoon by car they are often accompanied through the countryside by strings of horsemen, leading and following their vehicle. There is a race course close to the main city park where trotting races are very popular.

Kraantjespots

The streets containing the shops and hotels lead off the main squares, and a most coveted souvenir is an antique Groningen coffee pot, called a Kraantjespot. Zuiderdiep and Brugstraat have good antique shops and sometimes you can run one to earth. Some craftsmen still make these fine pewter coffee pots. They have curved legs to fit over a spirit stove, a pointed lid and a tap. The Kraantjespot is an indispensable item in the typical Groningen family. Nowadays there is a blue spirit flame under the pot, but formerly a little live coal kept the coffee simmering.

A genuine Groningen pot is made of pewter and cast in eight separate sections – the lid, the belly, the handle, the neck, the tap and the three legs. When these have been assembled it is polished on a lathe and hand-varnished. Some are decorated with flowers, birds or stars, but I prefer the plain polished metal. Coffee is prepared by filling the upturned lid with a level quantity of ground beans. It is served with thin cream. Lumps of home made candy on string are kept on the table to sweeten it. One is lowered into a cup and the coffee poured over it. The cream jug and sugarbowl which go with the pot are usually of crystal and there are also silver tongs with grips shaped like chicken feet for lumps of sugar.

The Kraantjespot has not always, however, been an exclusively Groningen utensil, for at one time it was used at Drenthe in Friesland and even in Germany. No one knows the origin of this strange-shaped pot, but suffice to say that the Groningeners have for centuries been good coffee drinkers and enjoy pleasant evenings round the simmering pot. Nowadays they are often kept as ornaments.

Hofjes

Groningen, like other Dutch cities, has not forgotten its old folk and three of its *Hofjes* are particularly appealing, although quite different. In

36 *The Groningen Kraantjespot complete with a crystal cream jug and sugar bowl*

the centre of town there is the Linhoffstichting, a modern cluster of small houses around a grassy courtyard with flowering shrubs and plants. Another founded in 1664 is called St Anthony Gasthuis; with a striking clock it is old and picturesque. Its tranquil courtyard is entered through an open gateway with sculptured figures, marble swags and other ornamentation. On its lintel is written:

Do not mock an old woman
No one knows his fate
From old age and death God alone is free
All other things change with time

There is a memorial here to those who died in the last war. It is a statue of St George and the dragon but in a different pose than usual. The Saint is not astride his horse but stands with feet apart and arms at his sides. His right hand holds the sword, the point resting by his right foot. The dragon has been vanquished and the Saint's head is bent in prayer. His arms and legs are bare, spent with effort. His robe hangs in graceful folds.

The third *hofje* is the Pepergasthuis which dates back to 1403 and still has five trellised asylum cells from the old days when mentally disturbed people, young and old, were just locked up until they died. The other little houses overlooking a square of lawn and flower beds have modern interiors. Each has a small sitting room, shower, bedroom and kitchenette. A main meal is served at lunchtime in a large panelled dining room at one end of the square for those who wish it, and across the hallway from it is a charming chapel. This is hired out on certain occasions for weddings and other religious functions.

Museums

There are several intriguing museums in the city, the main one being at 59 Praediniussingel. (*Singel* is used for street as well as *Straat*. A street alongside a canal is often called *Singel*.) This contains some archaeological finds from the province: local silver, pewter and bronze, a few seventeenth- and eigthteenth-century Dutch and Flemish paintings and drawings by Rembrandt, Rubens and Carel Fabricius. Carel Fabricius was a pupil of Rembrandt; he died young, when a powder arsenal blew up in Delft. It is a must for visitors interested in china for it has famous collections of ceramics from China and Japan. A number of rooms are completely furnished in different styles ranging from that of a peasant to an ornate eighteenth-century drawing-room.

The small and fascinating Museum of Shipping and Tobacco, housed in a seventeenth-century mansion even uses the attic for display space. Small flights of wooden steps, with shipshape rope bannisters, lead from one floor to another. You will see rows of ship models (including the three masters which carried Dutch goods overseas), anchors, sail maker's tools, charts, figure heads, navigation instruments, compasses and armaments. There are models of the ships that took such famous men as Tasman on their exploratory voyages. One room contains a modern ship's bridge with all its instruments and controls.

Then there is the history of tobacco with displays of pipes, tobacco jars, oriental snuff boxes, clay pipes, ashtrays, advertisements and moving models. It is a fascinating account which will, of course, have a greater appeal to smokers, although non-smokers may admire the beautifully-crafted pipes of horn, wood, clay and silver.

Haren

In Haren, virtually a suburb of Groningen, is the largest controlled-climate house in Holland. Here you will find such unusual bedfellows as banana trees, alpine flowers, pineapple plants, coffee bushes, roses and hibiscus shrubs. It belongs to Groningen University and is one of the most modern glasshouses in Europe. There is a tropical and sub-tropical hothouse, a desert house, a monsoon and savanna house and finally a cool house with plants which thrive in mountainous countries.

Leek

On the road to Groningen Airport, near Eelde, is Paterswolde Lake, a northern aquatic sports centre with a swimming pool and boats for hire. To the west of the city is the town of Leek which has the National Coach Museum. There is an amazing collection of vehicles of different types and sizes from state coaches to sports cars. Among them is an ornate carriage which belonged to the Empress Elizabeth of Austria, and others which were owned by Wilhelm, the last Kaiser of Germany. These are displayed in an old country mansion surrounded by spacious grounds, including a deer park where there is a tea room, a mini-golf course, swimming pool and camping ground.

The shell grotto here is well known, its walls covered with thousands of shells showing cherubs, fish, flower decorations and other fanciful motifs. Legend has it that long ago a chambermaid in the old mansion was caught stealing and was punished in a most unusual way. She was locked inside the grotto with great mounds of shells and was told to decorate the walls with them. She did not finish this task quickly; it took her 20 years! When she emerged from her prison she walked to Leek lake and was so horrified at her aged appearance reflected in the water that she committed suicide.

As well as the grotto and the deer park the museum grounds also have a children's farm, a vast rose garden and a small railway running through the woods. You can even be driven round the estate in an old-fashioned mail coach.

As you drive north of the city towards Uithuizen to see the province's loveliest castle, Menkemaborg, the route is full of interest. Perhaps the greatest boon is that the roads are excellent and traffic is usually light – a pleasant change these days. Trees fringing the road bend over to one side where the wind from the North Sea lashes them. Two or three miles (4 km) to the west at Weheden Hoorn is the Auberge St Hubert which is a converted farmhouse and can accommodate 25 people in its restaurant.

Warffum

At Warffum you will find an open air museum, Het Hoogeland, which is a reconstruction of a small old time provincial village. Buildings of historical interest in the region have been saved from demolition, dismantled and re-erected here. In an effort to add realism, some of the

37 *The National Carriage Museum at Leek*

houses are inhabited and a visit is rather like stepping back in time.

The Schutstal is a nineteenth-century barn, once part of a large inn which burned down in 1935. In the 1960s the Vrouw Fransen Gasthuis, an old inn, was moved from Groningen and rebuilt on its present site. In earlier times guests at the inn stabled their horses on the ground floor and went upstairs for their own board and lodging. This arrangement was very common all over Europe and can still be found in some old farmhouses. The idea is that the heat from the horses and cattle rises up into the living quarters and helps to warm them. Today an exhibition of sleighs has replaced the animals at ground level. The Schutstal also served as a pound where stray cattle were kept until claimed by their owners. Sometimes weddings and other festivities were celebrated here and this tradition has been maintained as the barn can still be hired for parties. Tea, coffee, soup and pancakes are now served there. Near the entrance stands a fire engine dating back to the beginning of the century.

Next to the Schutstal is an inn with a small grocery store at its entrance where tea, coffee, soap, paraffin and sweets used to be sold. There are two nineteenth-century coffee pots on the counter and, on the wall behind, a *poestbrad* (dartboard). It is the predecessor of those we know today, but the darts were not thrown but blown through a tube. The small sitting room is laid out as it would have been in a simple middle class home around 1900. One of two cupboard beds has been turned into a showcase. There are other equally interesting buildings and displays of medieval costumes. Each June a folk festival and antique fair are held here.

Local architecture
Continuing from this small town to Uithuizen to visit Menkemaborg Castle you drive by many mansion farmhouses which are a feature of this province. Easily guarded in olden days the main house, called the Head, is joined to its large barn by an elongated smaller house, called the Neck. Some of these mansion farmhouses have as many as three barns tacked onto their sprawling length. The barns are built of red brick which weathers to a deep russet colour. Note the unusual weather vanes which are in the form of horses, rather than the usual roosters.

Menkemaborg Castle
Built as a fortified manor house centuries ago, Menkemaborg Castle has a welcoming lived-in appearance. It is as if the family had gone out riding and would be back later to change and then join you for drinks and dinner. The rose gardens are picturesque in summer, and one of the outhouses on the estate has been turned into a restaurant. The castle shows the style of three different periods, fourteenth-, seventeenth- and eighteenth-century, and more recently has been added to in such a way that it is now in a horseshoe layout, built out over the surrounding moat. There are small corner towers in the forecourt, and the façade of the building is in Dutch Renaissance style.

Hunting gear festoons the Knights' Hall. To the right of this there is a drawing-room with walls covered in gold-coloured silk. A splendid clock is decorated with small animals from the stories of La Fontaine, and a huge Waterford glass chandelier hangs from the centre of the ceiling. Tables are covered with silver filigree work, little gun carriages, bon-bon dishes, tea services and other household items.

The dining room is on the opposite side of the entrance hall. The table is laid for a meal with Wedgwood bone china. Flowers form the centrepiece and there are napkins on the side plates. The sideboard has a plate of fruit on it and a tantalus with port and liqueurs. A Sèvres coffee set is shown to advantage in a wall cabinet and a smaller cabinet is filled with some exquisite pieces of blue and white Ming china.

The gun room has a strange chair made of animal horns, and the walls are covered with hand-painted linen dating back to 1725. They are hung with powder horns and beautifully chased weapons.

An eighteenth-century drawing-room, known as the Biedermeier Salon, has a welcoming air. The large fireplace is filled with freshly cut logs, and above it there is a painting by Herman Collenius. This artist is said to have produced all the paintings over the various fireplaces. Vases are full of flowers, and a chair is drawn up to a wine cooler where a linen towel is to hand. Tall candles are placed in the candlesticks with snuffers to hand. Desks are open and notepaper and quill pens are ready for use. A Venetian chandelier is suspended from the ceiling and the furniture is upholstered in golden velvet. You feel certain your host will suddenly appear.

William I once slept here and you can visit the guest room where he stayed. The Louis XIV bed is hung with the same golden damask which was draped over it in 1700, although it has perished a little in places.

Menkemaborg Castle can be visited before midday from Groningen and, if you lunch there, it is interesting to take a drive further north during the afternoon before returning to your hotel.

The coast road dykes

Of the many dykes seen in Holland, I found the triple system along this coast road the most interesting. It comprises three earth banks with spaces between, the landward, lowest, one called the Dreamer, and the seaward one known as the Watcher. The centre one is called the Sleeper. We drove through the Dreamer into the space between it and the Sleeper. After a while we came to tall open gates. These and others like them pierce the second dyke at intervals and can be closed in emergencies. Driving along the base of the Watcher we came to a village called Oudeschip which was once beneath the North Sea.

Walking on the bottom of the sea

Seeing the mud flats stretching for miles towards the sea brought the new sport of 'walking on the bottom of the sea' to mind. This is a fairly recent innovation which has many followers and, among the international participants, British tourists have made their mark. Those keen on this pastime leave the shore at Pieterburen 15 miles (24 km) north-west of Groningen an hour before low tide and start to walk into the sea, which sometimes reaches up to the waist. As the tide recedes the water level drops and gradually the seabed is revealed. The guides have compasses and lead their parties, sometimes 100 strong, some 6 miles (10 km) to the island of Rottumeroog. The clothes recommended for this exercise are shorts, sports shoes and thick socks. The trek takes about three hours. Those taking part usually return by boat from the island. Everyone talks highly of the experience which is 'just for fun'. A moonlight trek is said to be the best.

Boating and sailing

At such places as Zoutkamp in the north of the province you can hire boats for a new type of sailing. There are more than 300 miles (500 km) of narrow winding canals offering ideal conditions for holidaying on a hired cruiser or canoeing. All kinds of craft taking four to eight people are available. No yachting certificate is needed. You will quickly be taught such regulations as there are and the handling of the boat. You can sail on the inland waterways and really get away from it all, yet there are villages within reach where you can buy provisions. The only thing not guaranteed is the weather!

Appingedam

To the north-east of Groningen is Appingedam which, with its pretty canals, is sometimes called the Venice of the province. The Nicolai church has some lovely paintings and is early thirteenth-century. The Town Hall is renowned for its seventeenth-century façade, but most picturesque of all are the houses built along the Damsterdiep canal. For a change they do not face the water, but turn their backs, and all the kitchens are built out above the canal, their reflections resembling strangely shaped gables. They are a favourite subject for artists and photographers.

Ekenstein Hotel

This hotel has a fascinating history. In 1648, at the end of the Eighty Years War, Jan van Eeck, first mayor of Groningen, built himself a country mansion, later named after the Ekenstein family. In 1754 Onno Joost Alberda van Nijenstein bought the mansion as a country seat and changed his name to van Ekenstein. His descendants rebuilt it in neo-Gothic style, with a large English garden. It remained with the family until 1979 and was then empty for several years until it became a hotel, refurbished and with a new wing. It has 30 luxury bedrooms, one of which has a secret door leading to a passage which could be used as an escape route centuries ago. There is a gracious dining room and one of the public rooms still has authentic wall paintings.

Delfzijl

Beyond Appingedam, towards the coast, you come to the harbour of Delfzijl, the third most important in Holland, a fast growing port and ocean terminal. It is on the Eems estuary which runs into the Dollard Gulf and has an extensive ship building industry. Ships can go from here along the Eems canal to Groningen. The sea aquarium, above which is an interesting exhibition of shells, is well worth a visit.

There are many off-shore drilling rigs, but far more interesting than these is the Eemshotel. It is also off-shore built, like a stork's nest, on high stilts out over the sea. With land at such a premium one must admire this project. The building is connected to the mainland by a covered arcade and has its own yacht harbour. It ranks as one of Holland's most comfortable hotels and the guests are accommodated in a tower block.

Loppersum

Inland from Delfzijl and Appingedam is the small village of Loppersum which has an unusual medieval church with a sturdy fourteenth-century tower. The interior is most impressive. Nobles of long ago are buried here, their family pews still linked together with carved coats of arms. The Gothic vaulting is covered with frescos dating from the fifteenth century. Biblical scenes are surrounded with swags and garlands. When part of the ceiling was restored more beautiful frescos were uncovered. One is of St Thomas, the other of Jesus standing at the foot of a vividly bright rainbow. Part of the vaulting, with mouldings in diamond shapes, is called the 'Fishnet of Peter'. An aged long table serves as a simple altar with brass candlesticks at either end. In the centre there is an open bible flanked by a large pewter plate and jug.

Nieuwshans

Nieuwshans, close to the German border, was an impregnable fortified village during the seventeenth century. Its original name was Langakkershans (Long Acre Fortress) and it was completed in 1628. The battlements have long since been dismantled, but there are some remnants of its past such as its parade ground in the centre of the village, a few beautiful buildings and several relics in the museum.

For some time it has been known as the principal border town in the north of the country, being on national route A7 (better known as the Green Coast Road). Recently it has got into the headlines as the first and only spa in Holland. Neighbouring France, Belgium and Germany all have famous spas, but the Netherlands seemed deprived, until five years ago an archaeologist digging in the area discovered hot springs.

The thermal waters come from about 2000 ft (600 m) below ground and contain, among other minerals, iodine and iron. Combined with high salinity they have a revitalizing and curative effect. The new spa seems to have been born almost overnight, with ultra-modern buildings in an attractive setting. The waters are pumped up by the latest equipment, some flowing straight into a large outdoor pool, which maintains a pleasant temperature of 36°C (97°F). The pool can also be reached from inside the spa complex where there are saunas, sunbeds and massage parlours. It is open all year around and, after taking the waters, visitors can relax in adjacent rooms or out of doors. Tennis and other sports are available, but if you prefer to have a drink or snack there is a restaurant with ordinary or 'health' menus offering plenty of choice. An added bonus is that the spa is in the section of Holland where the landscapes are wide, the air clean and the rain anything but acid.

Several interesting excursions can be made from it, among them the old fortress of Bourtange and the castle-like Ekenstein hotel at Appingedam mentioned already. Some 40 miles (65 km) to the north-west is the crêche for seals, at Pieterburen, where baby seals abandoned by their parents are cared for and fed until they are old enough to be returned to the sea. The crêche gets an average of 60 seals a year and manages to save 70 per cent of them.

Bourtange

This ancient township was first fortified by order of William of Orange and dates back to the sixteenth century. It is entered from a picturesque road edged by a canal on one side where a large windmill, like a sentry on duty, is perched high above the walled entrance. Bourtange has been carefully restored to its original condition. From its cobblestone market square in the centre, ten narrow roads radiate out, like the points of a compass, to the ramparts and bastions, passing old canons *en route*. Small tree-shaded houses line the square, including two seventeenth-century officers' quarters, and just to make the tiny township perfect for visitors, there is an inn with a restaurant.

Friesland

To the west from Groningen, along the Green Coast Road, lies Friesland's capital, Leeuwarden. Although a stately Dutch city, with the customary slender gabled houses, Gothic spires and straight canals, it has immense individuality. Its big business is cattle and its vast covered cattle hall, the largest in Europe, can house 10,000 animals at one of the Friday markets. The black and white Friesland cow is famed for its high milk yield during its lifespan and when slaughtered makes good beef. Though Friesland cattle are shipped all over the world it is jokingly said that there are more cows in Friesland than people. On the seventy-fifth anniversary of the Friesian Herd Stud Book (kept to record the evolution of the breed) a bronze statue of a cow was sculptured by G. J. Adams in 1954 and today it stands in the centre of Leeuwarden, symbolizing a thriving industry. Its pedestal in inscribed 'Us Mem' (Our Mother) and rightly so for some 40 per cent of local people are somehow involved with cattle.

Leeuwarden is particularly interesting for Americans because it was the first city to vote Holland's recognition of the new United States of America; after this the Dutch loaned the young country $30,000,000. In

he Provincial House, 52 Tweebaksmarkt, a bronze tablet is inscribed
with the words:

> Memorial of gratitude. At Leeuwarden in the States of Friesland
> February 1782, the first vote was taken which led to the recognition of
> the independence of the United States of America by the Republic of the
> United Netherlands. Erected by the De Witt Historical Society of
> Tomkins County at Ithaca, N.Y. AD 1909.

Also in the same building there is a document which relates that Peter
Stuyvesant was born in Scherpenzeel in Friesland in 1592. He was
Governor of New York, and virtually its founder, and named it New
Amsterdam. His farm, Groet Bouwerie, gave its name to the Bowery,
one of New York's districts. There is a statue of Stuyvesant in Wolvega.
Rembrandt's wife Saskia was born here, as was the infamous Mata Hari.

Museums

The city's three main museums differ greatly. At 11-15 Grote Kerkstraat,
the Princessehof specializes in porcelain and Eastern art. It has a large
collection of Dutch tiles, together with some from France, Spain and the
Middle East. At 13 Heerestraat is the Natural History Museum full of
information on local flora and fauna and with two dioramas, a meadow
and a dune scene, as well as a mammal department and a very extensive
collection of birds. There are also smaller collections of butterflies,
seashells, minerals and fossils. The Friesian Museum at 24 Turfmarkt
contains Friesian works of art, relics and medieval costumes.

The geography of Friesland

The surface of the land in Friesland is only just above (and in some cases
below) sea level and inundations have been frequent. By a great feat of
engineering the Zuyder Zee on the west and north – now called the
Ijsselmeer – has been shut off from the sea by means of an 18½ mile
(30 km) dyke. As you drive along the top of this, on one side you have the
cold waves of the North Sea and on the other a calmer fresh water inland
lake. In the middle you can be out of sight of land and feel as if you are
driving along a tight but strong rope. The core of the barrier resists the
tides and the lake gets its water from the *polders* and rivers inland. Surplus
water is drained off through sluices at low tide and the fresh water is used
by the provinces of North Holland and Friesland.

Of the many Friesian crafts which flourish, perhaps the best-known is
the making of clocks which usually have outdoor or biblical scenes on
their faces, surrounded by cavorting cherubs. The cog wheels are locally
forged and the chains handmade. They are designed to hang on walls and
are weight-driven.

Pottery is distinctive – especially that made at Wokkum – and coloured with oxides of copper and cobalt. Scroll work is added either by a metal tool or squirted through a cow's horn rather like icing a cake. Hand-painted furniture is designed in Hindelopen with a mixture of local and oriental motifs.

As with most of the provinces, Friesland has its food specialities. *Suikerbrood* is a type of bread with a sugary cinnamon flavour. Small seed cakes are called *Dumkes*. *Drabbel* cookies can be bought anywhere, but came originally from Sneek where a special type is called *Haga*. The mixture to make them is shaken through a three-nozzled funnel into boiling butter where it solidifies.

As walking on the bottom of the sea has a great vogue in Groningen so, in Friesland, the tour of the 11 cities – 125 miles (200 km) in one day – is the great skating event of the year, although it is not always possible to hold it. Racing is announced when the judges decide that the ice on the canals is thick enough to withstand the weight of the many competitors. The race begins before daybreak and ends well after dark. Frost-bite and snow blindness are major hazards, and it is a gruelling course. Pim Mulier, a sports journalist, started the craze in 1890 when he covered the course in 12 hours 55 minutes. Competitors have to clock in at each of the 11 cities of the province, and nowadays they are watched over by a helicopter. In 1942 the winner covered the course in 8 hours 44 minutes. In 1947 the weather was so unkind that only 10 per cent completed the circuit. In 1956 a strange thing happened: five skaters were so close together that they came to the finishing point arm in arm. They were all disqualified and the sixth skater was acclaimed the winner! The 1985 winner was Evert van Bentum on 21 February, the first race to be held for 22 years.

Kaatsen

Kaatsen is a Friesland pastime which is played from June to September. It is a sort of fives, or hand tennis, and is supposed to have been played by the Ancient Romans. A good game can draw up to 15,000 spectators and the finals are held in Franeker in late July.

Pole vaulting

Pole vaulting over water is an unusual and hilarious sport. The Friesian countryside is criss-crossed by canals and ditches and the easiest way to cross from field to field is to carry a pole with you and vault across them. This has now developed into a sport and the annual championships take place in the village of Winsum. The winner is the person who vaults the furthest, not the highest, and the present record is $15\frac{1}{2}$ yd (14 m).

38 *Two typical Dutch trademarks – a windmill and a counter-balanced bridge*

Epilogue

One of the things that immediately strikes the visitor about Holland is the sharp contrast between the ultra-modern and the old. Rotterdam is a case in point. On the one hand there is the amazing Euromast overlooking the vast harbour and modern city centre. There is a building shaped like an aircraft wing, another like a beehive and yet more novel houses on stilts which appear to lean at odd angles. Once beyond the Lijnbaan shopping centre you come to old Rotterdam. Here is the St Laurens church in late Gothic style, built between 1449 and 1525. Reduced to ruins in May 1940 by bombs and fire damage, reconstruction began in 1952 and an accurate restoration was completed by 1968. Behind it stand the statue of Erasmus, his long robes brushing his feet. He reads his book seemingly oblivious to the existence of the torn nude statue *Destroyed City* erected to commemorate the bombing of the city in the Second World War.

Then there is Amsterdam with its core of magnificent seventeenth-century buildings rubbing shoulders with those as up to date as the Stedelijk Museum and the luxury hotels. Surprisingly often you get glimpses of the latest fashions mingling with national costumes and jewellery handed down for generations. You never know when you enter a café if the tables will be laid with linen or small rugs, the latter a remnant from East Indies days.

Whatever food you fancy all kinds are available including the famed Indonesian *rijstaffel*. Another unique aspect of Holland is the way in which the flat countryside is given interest and character by the interlacing of canals and roads, the former sometimes above the latter.

Music spans the whole range from magnificent concerts staged in splendid halls to barrel organs in the streets, nowadays driven by portable electric generators. There are many things to do. A new way to see Amsterdam's canals at their best and to linger where you wish is to hire a canal bike. It is a pedalboat seating up to four people. There are about four places in the city from which you can rent them. At night they are equipped with Chinese lanterns. Take along a little wine and cheese to enhance your journey.

The Dutch have prospered by being a trading nation and languages seem to come easily to them. Nearly everyone speaks some English, they enjoy meeting people and are ready to make you welcome. One thing is certain, once you have visited The Netherlands you will return again.

Index